The Journey to a Great Life NOW:
Achieving a Life with Less Stress and More Optimism, Happiness, & Success

The content of this book has been prepared for informational purposes only.

Published by Brand At Work

Editor: Sarah J. Singer Editing Services
Contributor: Josh Fernandez, Fresh Communications, LLC

979-8-9986969-0-9 paperback
978-0-9795875-9-7 ePUB

Printed in the United States of America

Legal Disclaimer

This book, its contents, and all associated workbooks and videos are intended for educational purposes and should in no way be interpreted as medical or any other advice. This book reflects the author's personal experience. The views, opinions, and advice contained in this book represent the views, opinions, and advice of the author, not the publisher. The author is not a certified or licensed healthcare professional. Because the advice, strategies, and recommendations contained in this book may not be suitable for your particular situation, the author and publisher make no expressed or implied warranties and assume no liability whatsoever, in connection therewith, including warranties about the type or extent of any benefits to be gained from attempting a similar regimen. The author and publisher recommend that anyone reading this book consult with appropriate licensed professionals and other experts before taking any action in connection with, or based on, the contents of this book.

Although the publisher and the author have made every effort to ensure that the information in this book was correct at press time and while this publication is designed to provide accurate information in regard to the subject matter covered, the publisher and the author assume no responsibility for errors, inaccuracies, omissions, or any other inconsistencies herein and hereby disclaim any liability to any party for any loss, damage, or disruption caused by errors or omissions, whether such errors or omissions result from negligence, accident, or any other cause.

This publication is meant as a source of valuable information for the reader; however, it is not meant as a substitute for direct expert assistance. If such level of assistance is required, the services of a competent professional should be sought.

Table of Contents

EXERCISE

In your workbook . . .

On this journey, you will be guided through a variety of thoughtful exercises, all of which are located in the Great Life NOW Workbook. To access your Great Life NOW workbook, visit www.greggledererman.com.

Once you have
self-worth,
you can move
mountains.

- Carol Lederman

The Inspiration

If you asked 1,000 different people what a great life looks like, you would NOT get 1,000 different answers. In fact, you wouldn't even get 100 different answers. What you would find is that certain answers show up on most people's lists. Most would agree that living a great life includes living with a sense of purpose, having fun, and having energy and focus that lead to less stress and more time to do the things you love with the people you love most.

However, too many people find achieving such a life to be quite elusive, and it's not because they don't want it. It's because they don't have either the recipe or the motivation. Through the Great Life NOW journey, I guarantee you will learn the recipe. All you've got to do is bring the motivation.

Allow me to begin with both a thank you and a congratulations!

Thank you for trusting me to be your tour guide on this journey toward creating a better life for you, your family, your friends, and those you interact with in the communities where you work and play. I'm truly grateful and inspired to join you on this journey.

Congratulations on making the decision to explore and implement what it takes to live a Great Life NOW. Whether you know it or not at this point, by taking this step, you are committing to living with a greater sense of purpose and with an energy and focus that will lead to less stress, more time, more happiness, and ultimately more success. This is what it means to live a Great Life, and you are starting it right NOW!

During our time together, you'll have the opportunity to gain tremendous insight and transform how you see the world and yourself in it. You'll learn life-improving insights that will have a big impact on how you think, feel, speak, and act.

In fact, if you are willing to open your heart and mind and to dive deep with me into who you are and why, I can assure you that you'll enhance your self-worth and move mountains.

Allow me to share with you the impetus that led to the Great Life NOW journey.

The story I'm sharing with you is deeply personal and explains some of the background that led me to develop the Great Life NOW journey.

My mother, Carol Lederman, passed away from breast cancer at the ridiculously young age of 32. I was an unborn baby when she was diagnosed and only two and a half when she died. My brother, Andy, was five.

As you might expect, her passing was devastating for everyone involved: me, my brother, of course my father, Norman, and all of our extended family.

For each of us, it was a very different experience.

For me, I have no recollection of my mother in my conscious mind.

My father remarried while we were young, my brother and I were adopted by our new mom, Donna, they had my sister, Staci, and we all lived a normal life in the Town of Brighton, in Rochester, NY. I say normal as if I actually know what normal is. Just know, it seemed normal to me.

I knew very little about my mom, "Mommy Carol." In the decade after she passed, I'd seen a few pictures and videos, and I'd had the opportunity to rummage through two boxes packed away under the basement steps that housed memorabilia from her life: some jewelry, more pictures, diplomas, and a few mementos that I'll bet were important to her but meant little to me at the time.

What I eventually learned was that my mom was a realist, and she knew the odds. She knew that she might not make it. After all, getting breast cancer while pregnant with me was a recipe for disaster as the hormones of a pregnancy only helped to spread the disease. But she didn't give up so easily. She battled for two and a half years until she lost the fight on June 5th, 1973.

Ten years from the time of her unfortunate death, I received both the surprise and gift of a lifetime. I'll never forget the moment Dad asked to see both me and Andy in his bedroom. He said he wanted to chat with us. Now at 12 and 14, if we were being asked to join Dad for a sit-down, it was usually because one of us had done something wrong. I recall feeling fairly confident that I would be found innocent. I took a seat on the floor in front of the bed, eager to find out what Andy had done wrong. It was at that moment that Dad sat down on the end of the bed and handed Andy and me The Letter. It was from our mom. On the envelope, it read, "For Andy and Gregg, to be given to them when they are ready to receive it."

Was I ready to receive it? I had no idea, but given that I had so little in the form of memories, I couldn't wait to see what it said inside. Little did I know at the time that her simple words would have such a significant impact on my life and subsequently, on the lives of many others. And soon, they will have an impact on you too.

My Uncle Mike is my mom's brother, and he was there with her during her final minutes. He shared with me that this letter was what was on her mind as she took her last breaths. "She was trying to tell me about a letter, but her whisper was so soft that I couldn't hear or understand her. The nurse came in, so I stepped out of the room, and moments later she was gone."

As it turns out, my mom wrote this letter six months before she passed away, hid it behind her wedding picture in the bedroom, and told only one person about it, my Great Aunt Bess. Upon my mom's wishes, Aunt Bess kept the letter a secret, even from my father. She would later tell me that my mother's message and instructions were quite clear: "I am not giving up, but if I don't make it, I wanted to write to the boys before I got too weak. If I don't make it, please tell Norman where it is."

My father was told about the letter and retrieved it about two weeks after Mommy Carol died. Today, I reached out to my father and asked him about the experience of receiving it. He shared, "I remember sitting in the bedroom alone, reading it. We'd all been through so much, especially during the first few weeks after she passed. I recall feeling inspired by how deep her thoughts were and was proud of her ability to write it. I knew at that moment it would be a while before I could share the letter with you and Andy. As the years went by, I realized I should wait until you were both old enough to process her message to you. So I held onto it for 10 years."

The letter did indeed house my mom's deepest thoughts. They were about life, her adoring love for my father, and her initial impressions of both me and Andy. She clearly wrote the letter because she wanted to give us something to remember her by, but also because it was her opportunity to provide some helpful guidance about what is most important in life and how to live a "rich and fulfilling one."

So, why am I sharing this traumatic event with you and what can it possibly have to do with you creating an even better life?

It is what was in this letter: a few wonderful insights, that at 12, were quite challenging for me to process, but eventually, sparked the motivation for my insanely passionate focus on knowing my core values and living them daily. And... helping others to know WHO they are and HOW to live it to achieve important, life-improving goals. All of what I just said, you will discover and implement as part of your Great Life NOW journey.

One insight alone made it impossible to forget my mom. It was a belief she held about what it would take to be successful in life.

Once You Have Self-Worth, You Can Move Mountains.

This quote immediately grabbed my attention and never let go. At 12, this was quite a deep insight for me to learn. Immediately, it hit me as an "instruction" for how to live my life. This instruction became my guiding principle and was one small yet impactful connection I had to the woman who brought me into this world.

As the years passed by, I'd regularly revisit the letter. During difficult or challenging times, I would hide away in my room, break out the letter, and get a quick reminder of what matters most in life. During my young adult years, I would wonder what Mom meant by self-worth. What kind of "mountains" was she referring to? Eventually, the meaning of both took shape and became hardwired into my brain.

What Is Self-Worth?

It's another way of saying self-esteem. The Merriam-Webster dictionary defines self-worth as "the sense of one's own value or worth as a human being."

Do you have self-worth? Of course you do. But do you have the right amount? Might you have too much, or not enough? How is your self-worth impacting your life today? How will it impact your life in the future? These are questions you will discover answers to along your Great Life NOW journey. You will not only explore what self-worth means to you, but you will also learn how to optimize it in ways that will bring immense satisfaction, optimism, and meaning to your life.

Back to those mountains. What did Mom mean by "moving mountains?" What were the mountains I should be moving? What are the mountains you should be moving?

Figuring this out took me into my adult years when I determined that my mountains were my personal goals, from relationships with my wife and kids, to career goals and personal well-being goals.

Unfortunately, I can't ask my mom if this is what she meant, but after reading the letter countless times throughout my life, I can safely assume, based on the context of her genius quote, that the mountains she was referring to had everything to do with the main areas of your life, that when optimized, create an even better life. A GREAT LIFE! This is the life she most definitely dreamed about for me, Andy, and my dad, even if she couldn't be there to guide us.

The concept of self-worth as well as a host of mountains to move awaits you in the weeks, months, and years ahead.

Enjoy the journey.

Welcome to Your Life, NOW

For more than 20 years in my consulting and teaching, I have pursued the answers to three questions:

1. Who are you?
2. How do you live "who you are"?
3. Why does it matter?

My curiosity has been sparked by a desire to better understand why some people are happy, motivated, and able to achieve more and why so many others… well, are not truly happy, lack motivation, and don't feel as successful as they want to be.

Through my own research and experiences, I've synthesized essential tools, techniques, and strategies to help people become better, more successful, and—most importantly—happier.

In 2010, after my initial design of the Great Life NOW, I began with my first client: ME!

Over the next five years, I worked the game plan I'd laid out while tweaking it until it was ready for use on other people. Then I began coaching others—in my Executive MBA course at the Simon School at the University of Rochester and with industry leaders looking to achieve more balance, happiness, and success. The learnings were vast, and the program became even better and easier to implement.

The Great Life NOW journey will get your creative juices flowing, and it will inspire you to get in touch with deep thoughts and exciting possibilities for what "could" and "must" be in your future. You're not embarking on a journey of things you "should" do. The goal is to design a Great Life NOW packed with thinking and actions that drive your "must" list of goals, strategies, and habits to provide you the life you truly desire and deserve.

In the past, the journey has been referred to as a program, with a start and a finish date. But there really is no finish date until the day you leave this world. The journey is a lifestyle that will impact the way you think, speak, and act in this great game of life.

As humans, we create the world we live in by the way we choose to see ourselves in it and by the way we act. Our beliefs shape our attitudes, both of which are daily choices. You can choose to focus on worry, fear, problems, and negativity… leading to stress and unhappiness. Or you can choose to focus on the NOW: being more grateful, feeling more optimistic and confident, while exploring more opportunities and experiencing more happiness on your journey of success. The best part of all is that you get to choose. Right NOW!

Life is a game, so you need a game plan.

Life is a game like all other games. The only difference is that most people don't realize they are playing.

Each of us has made up our own set of rules (our values) for this game. Whether consciously or unconsciously, these rules are based on our beliefs, and they dramatically impact how we play the game with our thoughts and actions (habits).

In order for you to compete at your best, you need to take control of the game, own it, and manage it. To do so means defining a game plan that outlines who is doing what by when, and that includes stated goals with a clear path to achieving them. A solid game plan needs to be simple and easy to follow, yet flexible enough to change course if needed.

> The Great Life NOW journey provides you the opportunity to create your game plan.

You'll find direction on how to optimally play this game of life... uncovering your purpose and leveraging your strengths. You'll discover what successfully competing looks like—how to eliminate fears, lower stress, and increase happiness. You'll determine the type of winner you want to be and how you want to go about winning the game through your values and the behaviors that bring your values to life. You'll develop more self-worth that will power every aspect of your life. Lastly, you'll design simple, daily habits that enable you to continue to compete NOW and for the foreseeable future.

Your game plan needs to be designed and then executed. It's your life. Design it the way you want to play it.

It's your life. Design it the way you want it.

This is your life, the only life you get, and you should make the most of it by designing it the way you want it. Doing so will optimize your happiness and outcomes. But you'll have to do some work to uncover what happiness looks like and what outcomes you really do desire.

I imagine some of you are thinking, "Not another self-help program packed with fluffy exercises, personal mantras, and daily affirmations." Trust me, this is different. True personal transformation requires more than positive thinking, or what I call "happy talk." You will discover that positive thinking alone isn't a substitute for taking action against social, mental, physical, and nutritional deficiencies that result from errant beliefs and poor behavioral choices.

The typical self-help program injects clients with willpower, which unfortunately dissipates quickly. In this journey, we will take a thoughtful and actionable approach to personal growth that balances past trauma and positive psychology to ensure you make meaningful progress towards peak performance in several areas of your life. You will learn not to take life the way it has come to you in the past.

Instead, you will be provided the tools to take charge of your life and design it and lead it the way you know it should be.

NOW is the time, and I am going to push you.

If you keep reading (or listening) and move forward with your commitment to this journey, please know that I am going to push you. I am not here to fix you. You're not broken. However, like many people, you fall somewhere on a spectrum. On one end are those who are a little misguided and lost, and on the other end are people who believe they are doing quite well on their own voyage through life. Whether you are on one end or the other, or fall somewhere in between, you will find tremendous value in experiencing the Great Life NOW journey.

My number one goal is to make sure you execute. Your number one goal should be to apply what you learn. That's a fair deal, right?

Learning the information will only get you so far.

Execution wins over knowledge every day of the week.

So, I will tell you what I tell every client: I will push you. That is my job. You may get uncomfortable being asked to demonstrate painful honesty. But trust me, once you do the upfront heavy lifting, the journey becomes easier and the benefits are amazing. Trust the process. It works. Don't be afraid to be vulnerable, and get out of your comfort zone. That is where you may find you'll do your best thinking and get the best results.

This is a multi-year commitment (just to get you started).

Wait... don't stop. Hear me out.

I'm just being honest. While designing your Great Life NOW may only take you a few days, weeks, or months (depending on where you are now and the time and attention you are willing to put in), the execution will be evaluated in years. While you should see results almost immediately with respect to how you think and feel, it takes time to make the behavior changes in your life truly habitual—to make them second nature. And it takes time to measure progress toward stated goals and outcomes.

So, I'm not offering a silver bullet or a genie in a bottle ready to grant you wishes for a Great Life NOW. The truth is, you need to do the work. But the good news is, once you get the ball rolling, the work is not difficult. And the best part of all, it is simple and easy, incredibly rewarding, and won't take you much time on a day-to-day basis. In fact, you will find your journey to a Great Life NOW will actually save you lots of time.

Oh, by the way . . .
YOU HAVE THE TIME!

If you are like most people today, you feel overwhelmed, with too much to do and too little time.

Your to-do list feels like a raging river… as soon as you get a few things checked off, what's waiting for you? Another wave of stuff to do.

You have what I call the Raging River of Responsibilities, where your daily to-dos (whether prioritized or not) are like the rapids of the river, flowing fast and furious. You have too much on your mind, too much on your plate. Your life feels somewhat out of control. You may even feel as if you have a few special challenges going on right now that prohibit you from investing in yourself.

You may be thinking to yourself, "Don't worry, the worst of it will be over in a couple of months. Then I'll be able to take a few weeks off, get organized, spend time with family and friends, eat better, and begin exercising. My life will be quite different then. I will then be able to create the positive habits that I know are important."

If you see yourself doing this, you're not alone! A lot of us fall into this same trap of planning for our future selves instead of our NOW selves. But it's also, frankly, bullshit!

Why? Because the Raging River of Responsibilities does not end. Thinking it does is, at best, wishful thinking. However, with the right game plan in place, you will learn to prioritize the most important activities that will help you decrease stress, live with purpose, achieve greater happiness, and be more successful in virtually all areas of your life.

It does take a little time. The key word being "little." As I already said, if you follow the plan, your efforts up front will save you time in the long run.

The logic of saving time will become clear as you go through this journey. For gosh sakes, just think about all the time spent dealing with issues you face in your life today—career, relationships, health and wellness, financial stress, and any others that drain your productivity and happiness. You will have the chance to address each and every one of these issues and either choose a new path that alleviates stress and saves you time or learn to be at peace, be happy, and move on.

Keep in mind, you have the same 1,440 minutes in each day that everyone else has.

Let's assume you sleep eight hours a day. That leaves 16 hours of awake time for work and personal time—960 minutes.

I am going to ask you this question now because I want you to think about it. You don't have to answer right now. It will come up again later. Then you'll need to answer.

Will you invest about 3% of your day to ensure the other 97% is truly GREAT?

Of course you will. Especially if doing so saves you time. That's it! That is all you'll need to invest to implement your Great Life NOW Game Plan: 3% of your day (approximately 30 minutes).

Why a Great Life NOW?

Because life is happening right NOW! When you reach the end of your pathway through this life, do you want to be "glad you did," or do you want to "wish you had"?

To reach your goals for tomorrow, first you must have goals. Next, you need to live each day (NOW) doing the things that matter most to your tomorrow. You don't want to get to the end of this voyage we call life with regrets that you didn't do all you could to be the best version of you.

Are you being the BEST POSSIBLE version of you?

My observation is that about 1 in 20 people (5%) are living a Great Life NOW—meaning they are truly living with healthy (and manageable) amounts of stress, an abundance of happiness, and a day-to-day feeling of being successful. Not just success as measured in wealth or status, but the kind of success that comes from a life filled with healthy relationships, where they enjoy their work, love their family, and like and respect themselves. The kind of life where people have the right mindset, take the right actions, and achieve their goals. All while being happy.

Beyond personal experience, here are some facts that shaped my observation:

- 33% of Americans are happy[1]
- 55% are stressed throughout the day[2]
- 45% feel a lot of worry[2]
- 83% do not have goals (goal achievement is linked to happiness)[3]
- 3% write down their goals[3]
- 80% of our daily thoughts are negative[4]

Those living a Great Life NOW don't simply want it more. They don't wish for it or pray for it to happen. What they do is the daily habits, often little things, that make their visions of a great life a reality.

At some point, they do the work to define what success looks like. That is exactly what you are about to do as you discover more of who you are, what you want, and how you can achieve greatness, NOW.

There's GOOD news and BAD news.

Good news first. Once again, the Great Life NOW journey is easy to understand, and the habits are easy to do.

Now for the bad news. Implementing your Great Life NOW plan will be even easier NOT to do. If you are like most, you've started and stopped diets, time management programs, meditation efforts, exercise programs, and other behavior modification efforts. Most of the time, people give up before they've really even started. Because it's easier to stop. It's easier to NOT do it. To just go back to doing things the way they've always done them. From my experience, too many people live their lives knowing they've NOT done important work on themselves that they know would make them better humans.

WHY?

Good news! A Great Life NOW is simple and easy to do. The bad news... it's even easier NOT to do it.

A key reason most don't do the little things required to live a Great Life NOW is because at first the results are invisible. That's right, you don't tend to see them right away.

For instance, the efforts applied to eating healthy don't materialize into weight loss or a better-looking body right away. In fact, in the short term, you may feel as if you are making little or no progress. The results are too far in the future, which is problematic in our "immediately, if not sooner" society of fast food, swipe right, instant access, one click, and just about everything at our fingertips.

We live in a world of instant gratification where patience may be a virtue, but it sure is difficult for most of us to practice, especially when we want—and sometimes expect—everything yesterday.

"When do you want those results? Immediately, if not sooner!"

Steve DePerrior

Sticking with our example, losing weight is not hard. Tons of classes, books, diets, and courses provide the simple recipe. Getting yourself to do the work is the hard part. You know what you should eat, but it's easier to eat junk food. Why? Because it won't kill you, at least not today. You don't have to exercise today either. Not doing so won't kill you… at least not today.

The same thinking applies to providing the extra effort at work, in your marriage, in your spiritual practice. In fact, this mode of thinking applies to just about anything you strive to make great in your life. If you don't do it today, you won't pay a price. But those todays add up, and before you know it, you are not only stuck in a rut, but you are not thriving by living a Great Life NOW. Instead, you are surviving in a stress-induced reality where happiness is sporadic and chaos has become the norm. You do not feel the pain in the moment of your choices, so they are easier to make (or not make).

> **"I do not need to communicate effectively with my kids today… not doing so won't make me a bad parent. At least not today."**
>
> **"I do not need to appreciate and recognize my teammates for their efforts this week… not doing so will not make me a bad leader. Not today at least."**

But what if you made communicating effectively and recognizing successes a habit that you invest a very small amount of time in each week (maybe each day)? What would that lead to? Would that lead to you being a better parent or a more effective and trusted leader? Of course it would.

I've just highlighted a few of the potential areas of your life that you may decide to make part of your Great Life NOW journey. Whatever areas you decide to focus on, you will learn the recipe for putting into practice the daily habits that position you to be an even better human, and a happier one too.

Where Are You NOW on the Pathway of Life?

The Great Life NOW workbook is available at greggledermann.com. All of the exercises from this book can be found in the workbook. Print it out or capture your responses directly into the workbook and save it to your files.

In your workbook . . .

How Many Days Do You Have Left?

Kind of a strange question to be asking, but it's important to know as you begin this journey. Let's figure out approximately how many days you have left. Take diseases, illnesses, and accidents off the table, and think about a realistic age. How old do you think you will live to be? Consider that the average life expectancy for someone in the U.S. is 78.6 years.

Fill in the equation to figure out your days.

How many days old are you?

____ X 365 = ____________

(your age) X (days in a year) = (# of days old)

How many days do you have in total?

__________ X 365 = ______________

(life expectancy) X (days in a year) = (total days)

How many days do you have left?

________ – ________ = __________

(total days) – (# of days old) = (days left)

FOR EXAMPLE:

If you're 50 years old:
50 x 365 = 18,250 days old

If you are optimistic and believe you'll live until at least 95:
95 x 365 = 34,675 (approximate days total)

34,675 - 18,250 = 16,425

You have approximately 16,425 days.

Your Pathway of Life

Most lives can be divided into three big phases with two fluctuations (flux points) between them, as shown in the Pathway of Life diagram below.

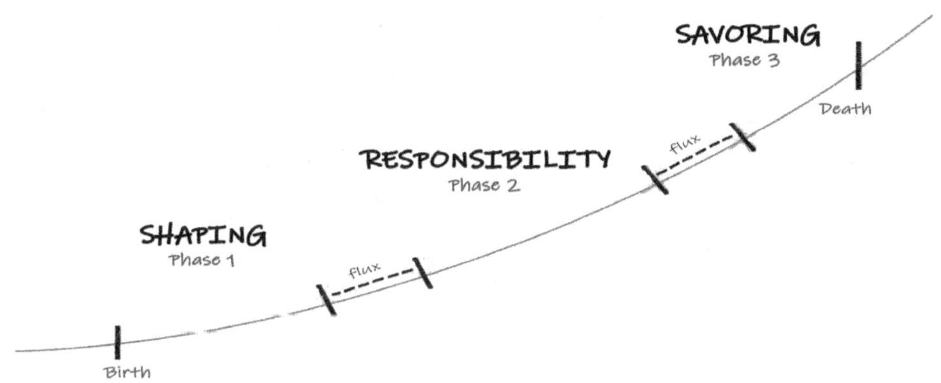

The pathway is sequential from birth to death and enables you to capture a high-level view of your life, both where you've been and where you are heading.

Each phase provides a very different life experience—and you will go through each phase at a different pace than others—but make no mistake, if you live a full lifetime, you will go through each phase.

Keep in mind, as you evolve through each phase, you become physically, mentally, and circumstantially a very different person. Most of us don't notice these changes as they tend to blend together, which makes the upcoming Pathway of Life exercise a valuable opportunity to step back and take a holistic view of your life.

Let's take a bird's-eye view of the different phases and use it to reflect on where you've been and where you are going next in your journey to a Great Life NOW.

In the first phase, you are completely dependent on others as you learn and grow. This is what I call the **Shaping** phase as you are under the guidance and influence of parents, teachers, coaches, and friends who help mold you into a young adult. During the Shaping phase, you start with very little freedom of choice; however, it grows over time.

Your teenage years bring the first of two fluctuation (flux) points where a shift in personality, priorities, stress levels, and choices takes place. The fluctuations happen between each phase and represent a period of about 10 years where new milestones are achieved. For instance, the first fluctuation typically includes milestones such as graduating from school and entering the full-time work world. A significant shift in accountability for choices takes place, and you most likely became much less dependent on others.

The second phase is the **Responsibility** phase. Others are dependent on you as you work to provide for yourself and/or your family. Your personality and work ethic have developed, but you still have a need for personal development and growth. While you may find this phase adventurous, packed with newfound freedom to make life-altering choices (such as where to live, what to do for work, and who to spend time with), you may also find that you're taking on more stress and burdens.

The Responsibility phase is packed with many difficult choices, which makes it critical for you to be able to prioritize your energy and focus to make optimal decisions, the kind of decisions that make for a Great Life NOW. I've found that those who cannot prioritize become overwhelmed and struggle to find balance, harmony, and joy at this stage of life.

Savoring is the third phase, and in most cases, it is the complete opposite of the second phase. There tend to be fewer big decisions, fewer responsibilities, and less daily stress. Different challenges, such as health issues and a lack of belonging, tend to increase during this phase. However, in most cases, others are no longer dependent on you, and you may no longer have to work, or at least you can work less.

The fluctuation years between Responsibility and Savoring may lead to a number of transitions depending on your desire to keep working, your physical, mental, and financial well-being, and the relationships you have in your life. When you create and activate your Great Life NOW Game Plan, you'll increase the probability of having more choices in the way you transition into phase three.

Once you get there, you'll find you are free to enjoy life with more desirable levels of flexibility. You are savoring life. You earned it!

Like I said, everyone goes through these phases at a different pace and can have wildly different experiences.

Trauma is another aspect of our lives that has, and will continue to have, great impact. Nearly everyone faces it, yet to varying degrees. From my experience, trauma can be attributed to a horrific event, such as a death, rape, or murder to a less, yet still traumatic, unkind word or personal embarrassment.

No doubt about it, trauma has an impact on your soul and your personality, and will therefore impact your journey forward. This next exercise gives you the opportunity to explore where you've been, why, and where you desire to go next.

Warning: Curiosity and vulnerability will be required to truly optimize your pathway forward. Get ready to dig deep.

Let's get into the exercise of exploring the Pathway for your Great Life NOW.

In your workbook . . .

Pathway of Life

The Pathway of Life exercise gives you an opportunity to tell the story of your life while also providing a guide to help facilitate thinking and goal setting for the next steps and phases of your journey.

Consider this exercise a warm-up to help you acknowledge and appreciate what has been—and feel excited about the possibilities in your future.

Demonstrate vulnerability while you explore difficult times and circumstances. Be curious to know how they've impacted who you are today.

Each step in the exercise is designed to help you:

1. Reflect on where you are and how far you've come.
2. Envision where you want to go and what you want to achieve.
3. Consider whose help you may need and who you can help along the way.

Where are you **NOW** on the Pathway of Life?

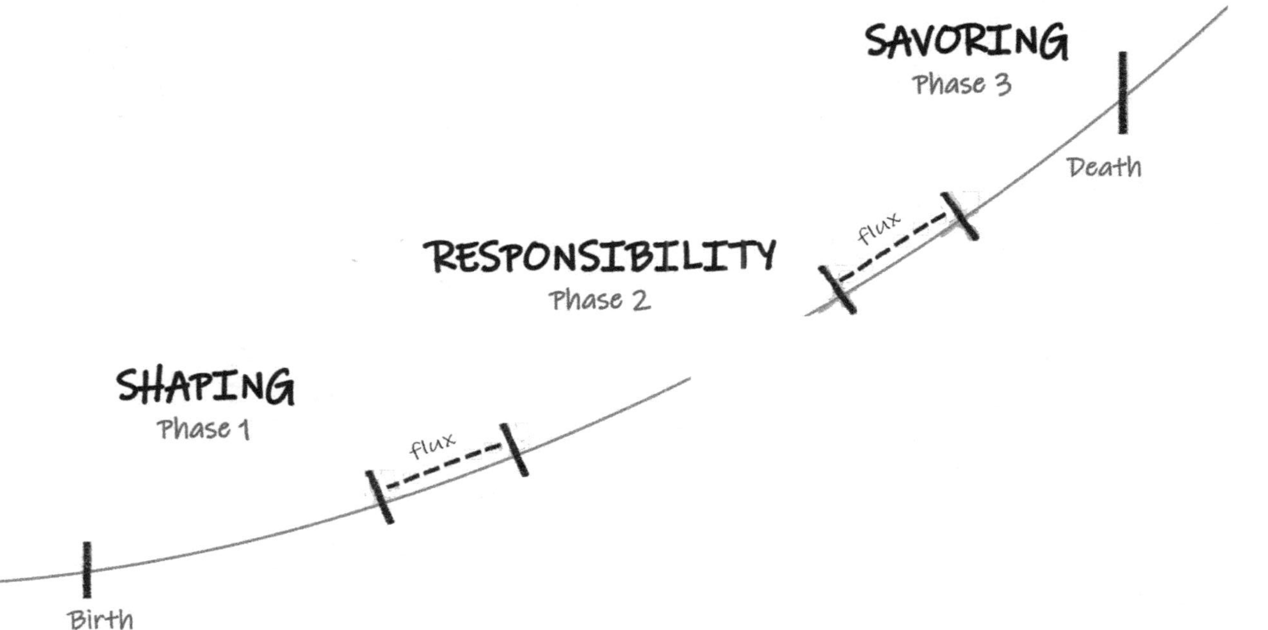

1. Make a note of where you are on the Pathway of Life.
2. Make note of important people in your life—kids, parents, spouse, close friends, boss—and where they are on the Pathway.
3. Backfill important choices and milestones along the way to where you are now, i.e., graduations, relationships, jobs, wedding, etc.
4. Think back through your life. List any traumatic experiences you've faced.
5. Consider the next 5, 10, or 15 years. What are some goals and milestones you'd like to achieve along the way?
   - Write down your goals and the key steps or milestones you'll need to hit along the way.
     - Goals are milestones, achievements, or anything you'd like to accomplish. They could be relationship goals (start a family), financial goals (pay off that student debt), community goals (volunteer with a cause special to you), career goals (get a degree), or something more personal (learn guitar). Your goals can be anything that brings a sense of happiness and achievement to your life.
   - If it's difficult to visualize what you've not yet experienced, reach out to someone who has achieved the goal and ask them about it.
6. Use the notes section to jot down anything you have found interesting, concerning, or surprising about your life so far or with respect to future possibilities.

Once your Pathway is complete, keep it nearby so that you can reflect on it over the years and record your progress along with the challenges, twists, and turns that will naturally take place.

The Pathway of Life you complete here will help you put your life into perspective and get you primed for the next steps in developing your Great Life NOW Game Plan.

The Power of One Percent

For things to change, you have to change!

If you want to see improvement in your life—your relationships, your career, your finances, your health—well, then you have to get better. It's as simple as that.

Once again, the good news is that every step of the Great Life NOW journey is simple and easy to understand and do.

The bad news: it's easier NOT TO DO IT!

Imagine if you added a penny a day to each area of your life that is important to you. (Don't worry, we will be diving deep into what is most important to you very soon.) But just picture adding a penny a day by doing one simple, daily habit in each area of your life that you feel would improve your happiness. For instance, a penny a day to improve a relationship, your health, your finances, your physical fitness, your knowledge in a specific area.

In each of these areas that are important to you, you add one cent daily. That penny would be applied based on little, simple, daily habits disguised as kind words, study sessions, workouts, etc. How much do you think you would earn (achieve) in each category? Could you double your earnings—that is, your skill level or your achievement? In fact, you'd more than triple the amount of success in whichever category you invest yourself in. More than triple!

Here's how it works… that one cent a day is one-hundredth of a dollar. That is equal to 1% of a dollar. So, let's say you add 1% to whatever habit you want to improve in the next 12 months. By the end of this one-year period, by adding 1% each day—pure addition, no compounding interest—how much have you added? A total of 365%. In other words, you've progressed by an amount of more than three-and-a-half. Now that's progress. And, as you'll learn in Part 1: Pregame, progress is the fuel for happiness, which ensures a Great Life NOW.

So, the question is not whether the effort you put into designing a Great Life NOW will pay off, the question is, how much will it pay off? And that is completely up to you.

Now, I'm not assuming you aren't already working hard or have worked hard in the past at improving in these important areas of your life. Actually, considering that you've read (or listened) this far, I think I can assume you've worked hard in the past and had some success, as well as some adversity, in improving in certain areas of your life. Why? Because you are a human, and we all face challenges in personal development. But I'm also going to assume you haven't embarked on a journey as simple and powerful as the Great Life NOW, which is uniquely designed to help you achieve personal growth NOW without a lot of extra work. No one I know wants to work twice as hard as they already are.

As you go through the Great Life NOW journey, please keep this big idea in mind: Successful people do what unsuccessful people are not willing to do. And they do it with small amounts of effort, as little as 1% each day.

So, do you think you could improve yourself—your health, your wealth, your happiness, your relationships, your knowledge, whatever area of your life you believe deserves the most focus and energy? Do you think you could improve by 1% each day?

Of course you can!

Let's begin the process of taking your life to the next level!

Successful people do what unsuccessful people are not willing to do.
And they do it with small amounts of effort, as little as 1% each day.

**If you fail to plan,
you are planning to fail.**

— Ben Franklin

1

PREGAME

Time to GET OFF Someday Island

Your happiness exists in one time—right NOW—and in one place—inside of you.

If you are on Someday Island, NOW is the time to get off. How do you know if you're on it? Well, for example, if you have ideas or ambitions you want to accomplish, but you have built excuses for not taking action, then you are most likely on Someday Island. Many people on Someday Island feel they will be happy later on, when something else happens: "Someday I'll do this and be happy. Someday I'll do that and be happy."

For most, Someday never really comes.

In your workbook . . .

NOW's the time to get off Someday Island.

Those living on Someday Island consciously (or unconsciously) tell themselves, "I'll be happy when…." We all do it—sometimes in small, seemingly insignificant ways and sometimes in giant, life-altering ways.

I've heard this called the "I'll be happy when" syndrome. What causes this? Billions of dollars are spent every year by marketers to make you feel like your life is incomplete right now, but you will be happier when you get (fill in the blank). These marketers are not bad people. Their efforts enable their companies to make more money. So, we don't have to beat ourselves up over it, but we should be aware.

I'll be happy when …

- I find that mate.
- I buy that car.
- I hire another employee.
- I close that deal.
- I have that skill.
- I lose that weight.
- I have the time.
- I make more money.
- I quit this job.
- I have that baby.
- I eat that_____.

What can you add to the list?

The problem is, whatever appears in that blank for you will quickly be replaced by something else the moment you get the thing you wanted. We live in a culture that falsely believes you can acquire your way to happiness. You may already know from experience that lasting happiness is not found in specific accomplishments. Maybe you've wanted something, but when you achieved it, the thrill from the accomplishment faded fairly quickly. The achievement may have given you a buzz of joy, but it didn't translate into lasting happiness.

You can't acquire your way to happiness.

If there is a pot of gold at the end of the rainbow, is that what we really want?

Most residents on Someday Island suffer in the present because of the alleged payoff in the future—the mythical Pot of Gold. There are a lot of problems with this, most notably that when you get to that pot of gold, you might find out it isn't really the one you wanted.

Let's say you live on Someday Island thinking you will be happier once you earn a certain amount of money to secure your future. So, you put all your energy into working and climbing the corporate ladder, and after years of body-depleting stress, broken relationships, and constant personal sacrifices, you make millions of dollars.

Uh-oh. Do you know where this is going?

Did you achieve your goal of making a lot of money? YES! Did you reach your desired level of happiness? NO!

Now you realize that it wasn't actually money that was going to make you happy, and you remain stranded on Someday Island.

It is as if you pinned your happiness to reaching the top of a mountain. Then you got to the top, and while the view was beautiful at first, and you felt a momentary happiness for how far you'd come, you also started to see all the other peaks you haven't climbed yet. Peaks others in your network of family, friends, and coworkers have climbed.

Oh no… you want even more. So, what do you do? Do you hunker down and keep climbing, sacrificing your happiness and the relationships that fuel it?

Getting off Someday Island and breaking away from the thinking of "I'll be happy when" syndrome does not mean your desires, goals, and ambitions will go away or lessen in some way. Just the opposite, in fact.

In this Great Life NOW journey, you will have the chance to get off Someday Island and experience more motivation, more optimism and focus, and less stress than ever before knowing that happiness is not outcome dependent. It won't come from making more money, getting a better job, driving a fancier car, achieving a certain body weight, or finding the perfect mate. You'll discover (or rediscover) that happiness really is an inside job—and once you do, you'll be able to think and act with more purpose, confidence, creativity, and decisiveness than ever before. You will clearly see that happiness happens right here, right NOW, and in doing so, you will drop the illusion that happiness exists on the other side of any place, possession, person, or achievement.

Someday is NOW. Let's get after it.

Happiness is an inside job.

In your workbook . . .

Happy Birthday, You're 100 Years Old!

Close your eyes for a few moments. Take 10 deep breaths.

Imagine today is your 100th birthday, and your family and friends are throwing you a party. They've asked you to share some of your infinite wisdom about your life. They want to know your biggest accomplishments and your biggest regrets. What would you tell them?

Biggest accomplishments I'd hope to tell them:

Biggest regrets I'd wish I didn't have to share:

It's not too late.
You have a fresh start on life starting right NOW!

The Formula for HAPPINESS

More happiness is a top reason why high-performing people invest in the Great Life NOW journey. However, happiness remains elusive for most people. Go ahead and Google "Happiness in America" (or fill in your country), and you'll be knee deep in research studies depicting the struggles we face with achieving happiness. How much are we struggling? Consistently, the estimations state that only about 1/3 of Americans are happy. Currently, America is ranked 16th out of 150 countries based on the World Happiness Report.[1]

Is happiness the purpose of life?

Happiness is a broad term that describes the experience of positive thoughts and emotions, such as joy and contentment. As Aristotle put it more than 2,000 years ago, "Happiness is the meaning and the purpose of life, the whole aim and end of human existence."[2] It's difficult to argue with this definition, isn't it? A bit wordy, yes, but it still rings true today. For most, the pursuit of happiness really is the purpose of life.

Endless research shows that being happier doesn't just make you feel better—it brings a host of potential health benefits, and this is why it is a significant factor throughout the Great Life NOW journey.

Happy people benefit from:

- Stronger immune systems.
- More fulfilling and longer-lasting marriages.
- Fewer heart attacks and strokes.
- Living longer.
- More resilient personalities able to handle adversity better.
- Larger, more active social lives.
- More involvement within their communities.
- Less physical pain and inflammation.

Of course you want these benefits and many more. But before we dive further into how to create more happiness, let's first acknowledge and get out of the way a few lies we tell ourselves.

A few lies we tell ourselves about happiness...

Lie #1: My genetics determine my happiness. Yes, happiness is hereditary, but only up to a point. Research tells us that 50% of our happiness comes from our genetic makeup.[3] Therefore, you can't use genetics alone as an excuse for continued unhappiness. Just because your mom or dad chose to be miserable and unhappy doesn't mean you have to. Those cards you've been dealt only make up half your hand.

Lie #2: My life circumstances are a primary driver of my happiness. The notion that if only something about your current life situation were different, then you'd be happy is a perfect example of the "I'll be happy when" syndrome that keeps people stuck on Someday Island. And it's a lie. The reality is, only about 10% of our happiness is circumstantial, meaning only a fraction is influenced by differences in life situations such as whether you are rich or poor, healthy or unhealthy, beautiful or more ordinary looking, married or divorced, etc.[3]

Lie #3: I can't control my happiness. Social scientists who've studied happiness for decades have proven that about 40% of our happiness is within our control.[3] You can increase or decrease your happiness based on how you think, speak, and act in your daily life. This is fantastic news. It means that all of us could be a great deal happier if we carefully inspected the thoughts we have and behaviors we do (as well as what other people think and do) that lead to more consistent happiness. Happiness really is a choice, and you control that choice.

I've observed, and social scientists have reported, behavioral patterns of people who are happier and considered successful. Happy and successful people tend to:

- Invest their time with family and friends. They are committed to nurturing those relationships.
- Practice gratitude.
- Give to others. They are typically the first to offer a helping hand.
- Be optimistic when imagining their futures.
- Focus their energy on living in the present.
- Exercise habitually.
- Have ambitions and goals and commit to achieving them.
- Remain poised and courageous when facing life's challenges and setbacks.

This is not a complete list. But it's a solid start to exploring the actions of happy and successful people.

One important point to make here is that success is not the key to happiness. It is the other way around. Happiness is the key to success. This idea is often a surprise to some people and, I must admit, is one that took me a little time to agree with.

Those stuck on Someday Island may believe that success will lead to more happiness. Again, I can't emphasize enough that this is not how it works. Once you do what it takes to increase your happiness, you will then become more successful, healthier, less stressed, and more likely to achieve the results you desire. Happiness comes first. Just think, is there any failure in life greater than achieving success without happiness? What's the point?

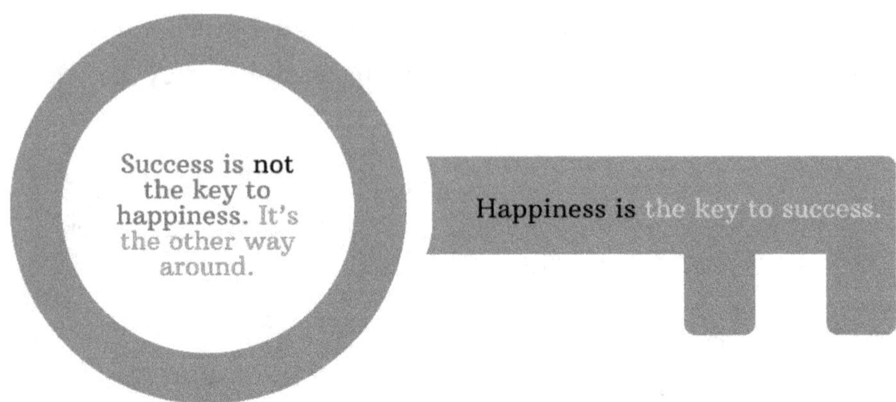

Okay… so if success does not lead to happiness, then how do we generate more happiness? It starts with a choice. The most important choice you will ever make.

The most important choice of your life.

You have one choice in life that is more important than all others, and it is not about your career, mate, or religion. Those are important choices, and you've made many of them and will have many more to make in the future. But in the end, you can toss out all those choices and just make one basic, underlying decision: Do you want to be happy, or do you not want to be happy?

However, if you are like many, you do not give yourself that choice because you believe it is out of your control. You might say, "Well, of course I want to be happy, but I am 30 pounds overweight and can't seem to stop eating," or "My husband left me," or "I lost my job." In other words, you want to be happy, but not if you are overweight, or not if your husband left you. You want to be happy, but you can't right now because you lost your job.

Let's revisit the question, which is a very simple one: "Do you want to be happy or not?" If we keep the question this simple, you'll see that it really is under your control; it's just that you have a deep-rooted propensity to qualify your happiness with things you can't control.

No question about it... your happiness is under your control.

Happiness is a simple equation.

Happiness is experienced consistently on the Great Life NOW journey when your results match your expectations.

For each day, week, and month along the way, you'll experience accomplishments and occasional failures. Both have an impact on your happiness to different degrees. But it's typically not the accomplishments and failures themselves that most impact your happiness level. Instead, it's the **habits** that lead to success and the **progress** you've made, even in the face of failure.

The secret formula for happiness:

HABITS + PROGRESS =

HAPPINESS

In the Great Life NOW Game Plan, you'll lay out your expectations for how you want to live your life and what you'd like to achieve. The inputs to this Game Plan are set up in a manner to help optimize your success. During each step in the last phase of the Great Life NOW journey (Activation), you'll need to act on daily, weekly, and monthly habits to lead you down the right path. Along the way, you'll be conditioned to pay attention to small wins and accomplishments—quite simply, the progress that you are making. Ever hear the saying, “It’s the journey, not the destination”? Well, it’s true, the journey is packed with the little things you learn to do consistently that fuel your progress, and when you pay attention to that progress, you become happier.

We can’t ignore the fact that you’ll also experience adversity in the form of twists and turns, and, on any given day, your life may not match your expectations, and you might feel unhappiness or pain. Sometimes you might even see a large gap between your reality and the expectation you’ve put into your Game Plan, in which case, you may experience extensive stress, anxiety, and unhappiness.

I’m sharing this as I don’t want to mislead you into thinking you simply make the choice to be happy, then you come up with some habits that will lead to your desired goal, and then all you have to do is pay attention to progress, and voila, you are happy!

One thing you can count on is that at times, life just won’t match how you think it should be. You’ve laid out your Game Plan, and now you’ve been dealt a few circumstances that seem to change everything. Adversity has reared its ugly head. What are you to do?

When adversity strikes (and it will), you typically have three choices:

1. **Blame** someone or something—the Blamestorm. This tends to create anger, can be toxic, and may destroy your spirit. (Not recommended.)

2. **Choose** to do something different.

3. **Change** your Game Plan.

From my experience, the best option is usually a combination of choosing to do something different and changing your Game Plan.

The secret to **HAPPINESS**
is to **WANT** what you **HAVE** ...

... while you **PURSUE**
what you **WANT**.

In your workbook . . .

What Does Happiness Look Like Right NOW?

These five questions are designed to get you started exploring happiness in your life. They will provide further insight to help you in developing your Game Plan in Part 2 of the Great Life NOW.

What areas of your life are you happy about?

Why are you happy with these areas of your life?

What is one thing you are not happy with?

Why are you not happy with this one thing?

What might you consider doing differently in the future that will bring you more happiness?

What Do You F.E.A.R.?

Fear is a distressing emotion that causes you to feel frightened, regardless of whether you should be afraid or not. The key word here is *regardless*, which means that it's possible (and likely) you will feel fear even when you shouldn't be scared.

Fear is part of our evolutionary survival mechanism known as "fight or flight," dating back to the prehistoric days when early humans needed to protect themselves from physical harm caused by wild animals or other humans. In a dangerous or stressful situation, our bodies are designed to release the hormone cortisol, which triggers our fear response.

Today, nearly all of our day-to-day fears are non-physical, meaning they only exist in our heads, such as fearing people or places and experiencing emotional insecurities. Unfortunately, we humans worry a lot. We always have, and sadly, we always will. But that doesn't mean YOU have to let it control your thinking and impact your stress level and happiness.

> **"Ninety-nine percent of the things I worried about never happened."**
>
> — Dale Carnegie

In his 1944 book, *How to Stop Worrying and Start Living* , Dale Carnegie shared, "I discovered that ninety-nine percent of the things I worried about never happened." [4]

Well, as it turned out, Carnegie's revelation from decades ago is still true today. Experts estimate that 99 out of 100 things we worry about never come to pass.

Think about this for a moment. 99% or more of the distressing emotions we stimulate inside ourselves may never come to pass. This reality has helped me embrace an acronym for FEAR: False Evidence Appearing Real. I'm not suggesting you should never be fearful. I'm just trying to provide some perspective.

Let's take a moment to process a few of your fears and determine how many were actually False Evidence Appearing Real (F.E.A.R.).

F.E.A.R.

What were your biggest worries…

How many of these worries have materialized in your life?

Just think—what if you stopped worrying about what might happen tomorrow… wouldn't that free up more energy to actually enjoy today?

This is easier said than done. Most of us have little awareness of the thoughts running through our heads.

Our negativity breeds more fear.

Many of us stroll through our day, listening to the "voice of fear" and allowing it to influence our choices. We humans have anywhere from 12,000 to 60,000 thoughts a day, and research indicates that nearly 98% are the same thoughts as the day before.[5] This wouldn't be so bad except that researchers have also uncovered that approximately 80% of those thoughts are negative, and negative thoughts are synonymous with fear-based thoughts. Do you see where I am going with this?

This means that nearly 80% of our thinking is being influenced by the voice of fear. You might be thinking, "You can't be serious!"

I am.

If you stop worrying about what might happen tomorrow, you're free to enjoy more of today.

And this is why, as part of the Great Life NOW journey, you must process your fears and get to the truth about them—the truth about **what** you fear and **why** you fear it. In addition, you'll want to consider how your fears help you. And, most importantly, consider how they might be hurting you. Doing so may not be easy, but it is necessary to enable your growth as a human. Not getting to the truth about fears will most likely increase your stress, block you from happiness, and hinder your growth.

The truth about fear.

Let's begin with the truth about fears in general. We cannot escape fear. We also don't want to let it hold us back. Your goal should be to transform fear into a friend that joins you on your journey through a Great Life NOW.

Some people have told me that they are never afraid, yet when I question them, they reveal that we are just differing on semantics. Yes, they feel nervous or anxious sometimes—they simply don't label it as fear.

From my experience, everyone feels fear as they move through life. I can imagine it is possible there are some evolved souls in this world who never experience fear, but I certainly have not met them. If I ever do, I promise to learn their secrets and report back to you.

Below are three truths to keep in mind about fears before you dive into exploring your reality of fear.

TRUTH 1: If you are growing, you will face fear.

Everyone faces fear, especially when in unfamiliar territory. Celebrities and star athletes didn't get to where they are without facing their fears. You may think they are lucky because they aren't afraid to put themselves out there. Not so! They had to push through a tremendous amount of fear to get where they are today... and they are still pushing.

For instance, Chris Evans, of Captain America fame, shared on ABC's *Jimmy Kimmel Live* that he was "scared" to accept Marvel's nine figure contract offer. In fact, on several occasions before the offer, he even turned down the role of Captain America, citing repeated battles with anxiety and panic attacks. In particular, he was fearful of the proliferation of internet commentary and how it would reflect on him and his work. It wasn't until a call from the Iron Man (Robert Downey Jr.), along with the persistent efforts of Kevin Feige (President of Marvel Studios) that he finally decided to take on the role. He is quoted as saying that it was the best decision he's ever made and not taking on the role would have been a giant mistake.

Evans made his debut as the comic-book character in 2011's *Captain America: The First Avenger*. He went on to star in many other Marvel movies, including the award winning *Avengers: Endgame*.

In a 2020 interview with *The Hollywood Insider* where he talked about his fears and anxiety, Evans said, "All the things that I was fearing never really came to fruition." [6]

Just like Captain America, you will experience fear when faced with unfamiliar territory, and so does everyone else. Once you face a specific fear, it will go away. But the reality of fear in general never goes away.

But just like Chris Evans, you can learn to move through the fear and crush it.

TRUTH 2: If you feel it and move through it, you will crush it.

This sounds contradictory to Truth 1, yet it isn't. Fears of particular situations or taking certain actions will dissolve when you finally confront them. The "doing it" comes before the fear goes away. I often tell my clients: Be like Nike and Just Do It. Crushing a fear means that you've moved through it, faced it head on, and become more comfortable with the situation. Unfortunately, once you've crushed one fear, you'll find it's like playing Whack-a-Mole—another one simply pops up as you experience new situations in life.

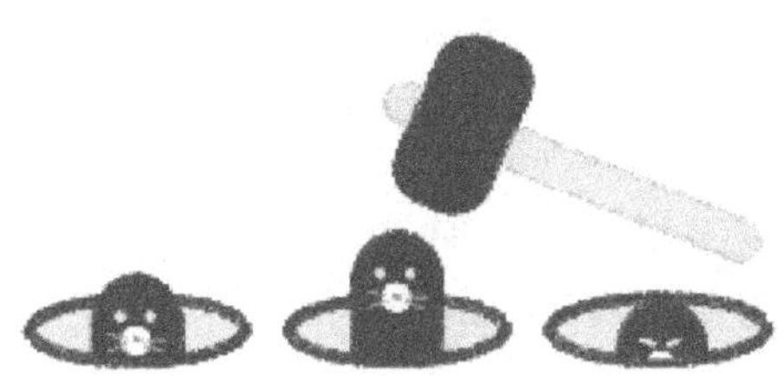

As an example, when I think back to my time as an MBA student in 1999, I was more than just a little fearful of speaking in public. I vividly recall a presentation in my Management Communications course. Even though I was in front of the friendly faces of my classmates, whom I'd been in school with for more than a year, I was still petrified.

I'd worried the entire night before, leading to a sleepless night. I sat in class, nervously awaiting my turn to speak. I had no choice in this situation as the presentation was required to pass the class. So, like everyone else, I had to "just do it." I got up there in front of my classmates, my knees shaking, my voice unsettled, and sweating profusely through the back of my shirt. While I survived this presentation, I can't say I felt much better about speaking in public. But I had made progress taking an initial step to overcome my fear.

I found myself in the same situation a few years later when I started my consulting firm, Brand Integrity. I had designed workshops as a way to help organizations define their core values and, in order to do my work, I had to speak to groups of people within the organization. Was I fearful? You bet. Did that fear continue to decrease from one client to the next? Yes, it did.

Then, after being in business a couple years, I was asked by a client to present the results of our work at their industry conference. While I'd become comfortable (whacked that mole) with small groups of 20 or so people, the conference audience included hundreds. Was I fearful? Yup! But again, I knew that crushing the fear was in my best interest, especially since each audience member was a prospective client!

My experience with speaking publicly is one example of how once you've mastered something and crushed the fear, it will feel so good that you will decide there is something else out there you want to accomplish. For me, it was taking on more speaking engagements with even larger audiences.

Each step of the way, I faced the fears and crushed them. Fast forward to today, and I'd say those fears are well behind me as I've made a career out of being a keynote speaker.

TRUTH 3: Crushing your fear is less frightening than living with the lurking uneasiness and the feeling of missing out.

Many people live a life of "what ifs." What if I get sick... what if I fail... what if my spouse leaves me... what if I make a mistake...? So, they refuse to take risks.

For the type of fears capable of blocking your growth as a human, the feeling of dread is often far more severe than what you would feel if you actually took the risks necessary to help you grow. Yet, like many, you are probably blind to those fears.

Just to be clear, I am not referring to your fear of snakes or skydiving. Those are fears that could certainly be explored further, but they won't hold you back from personal growth. However, when you fear situations that you need to be in (or at least would benefit from being in) to grow as a person, then you have fears to crush. On the other hand, if you are fearful of being rejected, and therefore don't make the effort to reach out and meet new people, then the lifetime of loneliness may be quite a bit more painful for your future self to deal with.

The problem is... most fears are HIDDEN.

Sometimes fear is hidden, lurking in the background, only to be seen if you really look for it. Fortunately, unlike a predator, it's there to help you. For instance, my hidden fears drove me to be an overachiever at work for many years. It wasn't until I'd racked up another major success at work that I spotted those hidden fears. And of course, I didn't find them alone. I needed a little help from my wife, Karyn.

I was driving home one day from work chatting with Karyn when she asked me an intriguing question that helped me uncover my hidden fears. My latest book, *ENGAGED!*, had recently climbed to number five on the *New York Times* bestseller list, my company Brand Integrity was recognized as a Top 100 Fastest Growing Company in Rochester, New York, we'd just won a new client with significant growth opportunity, my speaking career was booming, and yet something was wrong. I was feeling tired, stressed out, and worried about my health. In the past two years, I'd been hospitalized once for exhaustion and twice for kidney stones—both stress-related issues. On the call with Karyn, I was telling her about my day with a focus on my concerns and excitement for a new software product we were creating. That is when Karyn hit me with a question that would turn out to have a profound impact on my life: "Why is it that you are not able to ever stop and smell the roses?"

I recall sitting at a traffic light when the question came. Normally, I am quick with a response, but for this, I had nothing. After a long silence, Karyn proceeded to highlight some of the successes we'd had at Brand Integrity, as well as my personal successes. She said, "Your book hit the *New York Times* list, and within one day, you were on to the next big thing. You don't seem to ever take time to appreciate the successes along the way. You just jump right back into achieving more."

Karyn's comments struck a chord. I was surprised by how frustrated she was with me. But I was also surprised because I couldn't disagree. That's exactly what I did, and I did it all the time. The question was why?

After some time to reflect, I realized that my over achievement was fear driven. It was that voice of fear in my head telling me that I needed to keep going, in fifth gear, all day long to keep achieving more. More knowledge, more status, more client wins, more speeches, more income. More, more, more.

Why? It turns out, our deepest fears almost always relate back to a trauma from our childhood experiences. We all have moments where we learn to adapt by attaching to a fear, and then we overcompensate to ensure we don't have the unwanted experience again.

At the time of my conversation with Karyn, I determined that my constant running forward, rarely looking back, and missing opportunities to "stop and smell the roses" was caused by my fear of failure. After a few days of reflection, I realized that I was afraid of failing at work, failing as a father, as a husband, and as a friend, and I was running scared each day to do the things I thought positioned me for success in all of those areas. At the time, spotting this fear seemed like a significant breakthrough. Little did I know, I was only scratching the surface.

My fear of failure is not unique. Most experts would agree that fear of failure is the most common of all fears. Yet there are others that work in concert or alone, and they block us from achieving a Great Life NOW.

By exploring your fears, you'll identify the ones you most closely relate to, determine their source, uncover the benefits they have provided, and consider how to "free yourself" of them in the future. While many of our fears have benefited us over time, we still owe it to ourselves to be FREE!

My fear of failure benefited me by fueling my work ethic, which led to professional and financial success. That doesn't mean I should hold the fear forever. There comes a time when you need to free yourself of the fear because it really is doing more harm than good. It wasn't until I really began to dance with my fears that I uncovered the cost of my fear of failure and how it was working with other fears to hold me back, blocking me from what I wanted more than anything… more happiness.

Before we get to the second part of my story about crushing my fears, let's dance with yours.

"The only thing to fear
is fear itself."

-Franklin D. Roosevelt

In your workbook . . .

Exploring Your Fears

Explore your fears in a way that gets them out in the open where you can decide to either crush them or recognize they exist and will continue to get in your way. In this exercise, you'll identify and explore the truth behind your fears.

Step 1: List your greatest fears. Think about what keeps you up at night. Are there specific worries you consistently have? Do you have any fears that may be "hiding" on you that you could spot after some reflection?

Step 2: For each fear, determine how it has served you in your life. What are the benefits you get from that fear?

Step 3: What might the fear be costing you? Why should you consider letting it go… freeing yourself?

Step 4: What thoughts or actions would lessen the fear? What mantra or saying could you tell yourself that would alleviate the fear?

1. What are your greatest fears?	2. What benefit has the fear given you in the past?	3. Why free yourself of the fear now?	4. How can you free yourself (thoughts or actions)?
Example Fear of failure	Motivated me to work very hard, long hours for over 20 years.	I have way too much stress, which decreases my happiness and makes me less successful at work and at home.	Daily hour of power each morning w/15 mins meditation. Review family & personal values each day. "Nothing to prove, everything to share."

Not done yet! One more step.

Step 5: Dig deeper to get to the most prevalent fears. For each fear in Step 1, ask yourself three times: **"Why do I have this fear?"** Be like a five-year-old who incessantly asks "why." Ask again, "Why do I have this fear?" Keep writing down your answers. Do it a third time: "Why do I have this fear?" Write down your answer.

Note: If after three whys, you don't get to the truth—the root cause of the fear—then ask two more whys!

FEAR:

WHY?

Why do I have this fear?

Why do I have this fear?

Why do I have this fear?

Were you able to penetrate to the fears beneath the surface?

From my experience, there are a variety of fears within three different levels of depth when asking yourself "why."

Before we get into the different types and depths, let's take a closer look at my fear of failure. What I learned in my fear exploration was that it is common and often disguised as a fear of not succeeding in life. Just as they say beauty is in the eye of the beholder, so is success. The real source of my fear of failure was the fear of not *being loved* enough and not *being* enough.

"May your choices reflect your hopes, not your fears."

-Nelson Mandela

I was disguising fear of failure as being an overachiever, providing for my family, and creating opportunities for the families of my Brand Integrity teammates. This wasn't really the truth. It turns out a lot more was going on. I was scared. And what I thought was frightening me wasn't real. It was **False Evidence Appearing Real**. However, the fear of not being loved and not being enough was very real—and, as it turns out, quite common. My fears were floating in the Circle of Fears just like yours and just like everyone else's.

The Circle of Fears™

The Circle of Fears is made up of three different levels that are interconnected in unique ways.

Level I Fears are represented in the outer layer, which houses fears that are based on situations you face. Situational fears are nearly endless, and they're not hidden. You know them, and so do most people who are close to you in your life. For me, the fear of public speaking early on in my career was a Level I Fear. These surface level, situational fears always have a deeper fear beneath them, which you can discover when you take the time to investigate.

Level II Fears are a bit deeper and usually hidden. These fears are ego-based and driven by a person's sense of self-worth or self-importance.

In my work with students and clients, I've uncovered five typical Level II Fears that are a result of traumatic life experiences. These hidden fears are what create the most stress and worry in our lives.

1. **Fear of failure:** Includes feelings of inadequacy and rejection, and a belief that others are judging you. Leads to strong desire to prove yourself through achievements. May cause reluctancy to try new things due to lack of confidence.

2. **Fear of change:** Sparked by a longing for the past even if the situation no longer serves you. Causes people to become stagnant and miss opportunities in life. Can lead to feeling stuck, insecure, and/or resentful if you believe change is happening *to* you, not *for* you.

3. **Fear of intimacy:** Characterized as the fear of sharing a close emotional or physical relationship.

4. **Fear of being alone:** Also known as monophobia, loneliness fears come in a wide variety, all of which can cause anxiety and a strong desire for the comfort of others in order to feel safe and secure.

5. **Fear of loss:** Also comes in many forms… a loss of personal freedom, loss of health, loss of a loved one, or your own lost identity. Sparked by a feeling of uncertainty about the future and often a longing for the past.

Level III Fears are the most deep-rooted fears and are universal to all humans. If you are willing to continue digging into your Level I and II Fears, you will almost always uncover at least one of these universal fears:

1. I am not **being enough.**

2. I am not **being loved enough.**

Take a look back at your answers to the Exploring Fears Exercise. After challenging yourself with the three whys, did you come up with one of the Level III Universal Fears? If not, can you dig deeper?

These universal fears have everything to do with feeling secure and loved—two desires innate to humans that we are naturally fearful of not getting. And these fears impact who you are and how you act, which is why understanding them and getting to the reality behind them is an important step in the journey to a Great Life NOW.

Circle of Fears™

Levels I and II show examples of fears... what are yours?

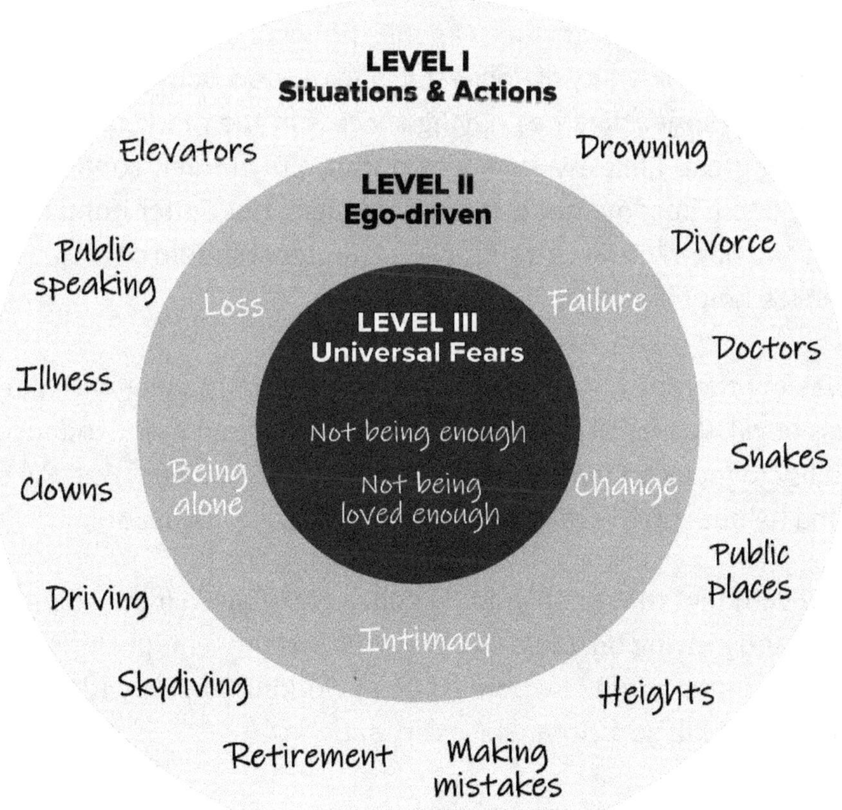

Now, back to my Karyn-induced exploration of my fears. She helped me see that failure kept me running scared each day, not stopping to appreciate the successes along the way. This was a Level II Fear, and soon enough, I learned it was not acting alone.

A few years went by and I found myself in the familiar stressed out and emotionally uneasy situation, only with a bit more awareness of this fear of failure. I'd achieved what I thought was the pinnacle of my career at Brand Integrity: selling the software business and having the opportunity to move on with a newfound focus on the activities I was most passionate about at work (speaking, consulting, and coaching). In addition, I continued to teach my course, Leading Organizational Change, to Executive MBA students at the University of Rochester, and my next book, *CRAVE*, was another award-winner that was having success in the marketplace. Things were going great. I felt my work was purposeful and felt confident I was helping people become not just better leaders, but better humans. I was content and happy. But not as happy as I thought I should be. At least, that is what Joe helped me see.

Joe was my therapist. At the time, I would regularly meet with Joe and discuss how I was feeling about my newly discovered independence and my ability to focus on family, friends, and the work I loved. But Joe could see (and helped me to see) that something else was going on.

I shared with him that I felt sad and guilty. I attributed it to selling Brand Integrity and moving on. I told Joe that I missed the relationships with my team and clients, some of whom I'd been working closely with for nearly two decades. I felt sad. Some days very sad.

I asked Joe, "With all of the continued success I am having in my post-Brand Integrity days, how in the world could I feel so uneasy?"

He did what most good therapists do and asked a question to make me come up with the answer: "Why do you think you have such guilt?"

I couldn't answer.

I spent weeks thinking about Joe's question. I sold Brand Integrity to a terrific organization that created a fantastic cultural experience and solid growth opportunities for my team. Knowing that most of the employees were in an even better place mattered a lot to me, and I was aware that my feelings of guilt were not over a sense of abandonment. And, as I said, I was getting to do more of the work I loved. I just couldn't seem to figure out what was going on in my own head.

At my next sit down with Joe, he brought up my childhood and began asking what I remembered about my mother. I shared how I was only two and a half years old when she died, and that to my disappointment, I didn't remember anything about her. He pressed me, asking questions about my brother and my dad. Joe was curious as to how we functioned as a family while my mother was sick and after she died.

Again, I had no recollection, but I shared some of the details that were told to me when I was older. I learned about the rotating door of nannies and family members who we no longer kept in touch with. In particular, my mother's brother, Michael, and my aunt Vicki. I explained that I was told my mother was very sick for the last six months of her life, with the last month primarily being in the hospital.

I shared that, after my mom died, we didn't see my aunt and uncle or grandparents (my mom's parents) for the next 10 years. I was told that they found it too difficult to be with us since their daughter (and sister) passed away. I was a young child and didn't question this as I had no recollection of them.

I vividly recall looking up during this part of the conversation and noticing something I'd not seen in the more than a year of counseling from Joe. He was tearing up. I was so taken aback by his emotions, and I could tell he was too.

Suddenly, the patient was becoming the counselor. I asked, "What is up with you? Why are you getting so emotional?" That's when I discovered the second Level II Fear that was greatly influencing my life: loss.

Joe looked at me apologetically and said, "You experienced such tremendous loss at such a young age. No wonder you are afraid of losing."

As I sat there processing his comment, I began to see it. "You mean the loss of my mother?" Joe explained that it was more than just the loss of my mom. I lost my connection to several people who were very close to me beyond my mother (even though she was clearly the most important)—my grandmother, grandfather, aunt, uncle, and a few nannies I most likely had become fond of.

At this point, I got a little uncomfortable with the conversation, so I did what I usually do, which is diffuse the situation with humor. "If you think that was a lot of loss, you should have been there a few years later when our dog Taffy died." We both chuckled as we acknowledged that, yes, I'd suffered tremendous loss at a very young age.

Joe went on to share his observations that just about everything I'd told him about my struggles with the fear of failing throughout my career and the unexpected guilt and sense of loneliness after selling Brand Integrity stemmed from a deep-rooted fear of loss (a close companion to the fear of failure—both Level II Fears and both connected to the universal fears of not being loved enough or not being enough).

We put his theory to the test and began exploring other areas of my life, including friendships, other family members, and the different areas of work I found myself absorbed in. Sure enough, the fear of losing was profound and driving my thinking and activity each and every day.

Is this a bad thing? No. In fact, just knowing it has freed me up to realize that, in some cases, it sparks a competitive spirit that energizes me, and it fuels my desire to invest in relationships that are meaningful. For instance, I have strong bonds with many friends from high school and college that I do not believe I would have today if my fear of loss was not a deep-rooted motivator. At the same time, if not managed, it causes me stress and unnecessary worry. Knowing this has helped me tremendously on my journey to a Great Life NOW.

How are your fears going to help you on your journey? How might your fears be holding you back?

We are what we repeatedly do.

— Aristotle

2

THE GAME PLAN

PASSION and PURPOSE

Passion is an intense emotion, a compelling enthusiasm or desire for something. Purpose is what you are determined to accomplish or attain in life. It is your passion in life that fuels your purpose. Not the other way around.

Early in my career, I was working with a coach (Bob) to help me with the direction of my business and my career. Bob sensed I was a bit undecided about a few viable pathways. I felt lost, as if I needed a sense of purpose. Bob agreed that determining my "purpose" would be helpful, but also suggested I first determine what I am really passionate about. He gave me two questions to answer and a few short minutes to do so.

1. What do you really love to do?
2. What do you hate to do?

At that time, I knew that I loved to engage with leaders and help them diagnose problems and discover opportunities. It was obvious to me that I enjoyed working with teams of people. I was also learning that I loved to present ideas and solutions to large groups. While my career was just getting started, early indications were that I truly enjoyed these activities and should focus on them for my career development.

For the second question, I was surprised by the word "hate" as I was taught (and have taught my children) never to use it because it is such an angry word. Bob insisted I share what I hated to do. The word alone sparked emotion and got me thinking.

My "hate" list at the time was short but specific and included:

- A pre-defined, rigid work schedule
- Dishonesty and selfishness
- Cloudy, cold, and rainy days
- Working alone in a quiet environment for long periods of time
- Uncertainty about what's next

After reviewing my list of loves and hates, Bob asked me one more question: "What are you passionate about?"

At this point, I was drained and didn't really feel like answering any more questions. Bob persisted, telling me, "If you don't know what you are passionate about, how will you ever know where to focus?" I must have looked a bit perplexed, because he continued, "You must know that where your focus goes, your energy flows."

This quote gripped me. Not just because it sounded catchy, but because it was so incredibly logical. Of course, if you focus, your energy will follow. I've since seen this quote in multiple educational areas over the years, so I know it didn't originate with Bob. Regardless, it helped in getting my energy flowing in the optimal direction.

**"Where your focus goes,
your energy flows."**

With this new philosophy powering my thinking, I became more motivated than ever to determine where my focus should be. I listed a few activities at work and in my personal life that I felt passionate about. It was a simple list of four or five things that gave me energy when I was doing them.

During this exploration, I realized I had a tremendous passion for learning, growing, sharing, and presenting. I knew I was on the right track in starting the Brand Integrity business as it provided me an opportunity to share newly developed expertise with leaders to help them achieve their personal as well as organizational goals. Little did I know at the time how much it would position me to take my passion to a much broader audience with a much greater impact.

Working with Bob to determine what I was most passionate about led me to create my **Purpose:** ***To use my knowledge and experience to help others grow and succeed.*** It may not be all that sexy, but it sure has kept me focused over the years.

Discovering my Passion and Purpose positioned me to make some very strategic career choices, such as developing my MBA course—Leading Organizational Change, which I taught to Executive MBAs at the University of Rochester Simon Business School. In addition, it is my Purpose that helped fuel my motivation to become an author and keynote speaker. If I left my decisions up to what I was most comfortable doing, I would never have chosen these pathways as writing and speaking in front of people were not natural skills for me to tap into.

Allow me to play the role of Coach Bob with you, and let's discover your Passion and draft a Purpose to guide you on your Great Life NOW journey.

EXERCISE

In your workbook . . .

Let Your Passion Fuel Your Purpose

This exercise is divided into four steps to help you find your Purpose. **Jot down** or **type** responses for each step.

STEP 1 : What do you love to do?

STEP 2 : What do you hate to do?

STEP 3 : List four to five specific activities you are passionate about.

These could be activities you do at work, with your family, or in your community, or they could be hobbies, sports, or any combination. Don't overthink it. Don't worry about the priority. If you feel stuck on whether you are passionate about something, skip it for now and move on to something that does feel important to you.

EXAMPLES:

- Helping a client solve a problem
- Taking a weekend trip with your kid
- Cooking a meal for a group of friends
- Collaborating on a project with coworkers
- Presenting your idea in a meeting

Uncovering your Passion(s) will help you live "on purpose," shaping your character and playing a significant role in ensuring you live a Great Life NOW.

STEP 4 : Decide on a Purpose.

What follows are a series of questions to get you to explore ideas for your Purpose. Read each question, then close your eyes and think for about thirty seconds about your response. Open your eyes, **jot down** or **type** your response, and then do the same for the next question.

What do you most value in life?

When you were a child, what did you want to be when you got older? Why? What was the feeling you wanted to have?

When you were a child, who was your role model? What did you admire about them?

Think of a situation in your life when things were really flowing. You were "in the zone" (also called the "flow state"). Step into that situation again.

- What were you doing?
- What were you feeling?
- Were you learning or doing something interesting?
- Is there anything similar between this time of your life and when you were young?
- What were you creating? Sharing? Feeling?

Next, write down ideas for the actions that drive your Purpose. Write something brief and emotionally charged. Describe how you're feeling and what you're doing. In your workbook, **write** or **type** as many statements as come to mind. The Purpose of my life is to...

From the thoughts you've created, **choose one of the activities** that means a lot to you. Don't overthink it. Go with your instincts.

Next, ask yourself, "Why do I do this activity?" This will help you get to the results. How does the action (activity) help others? What is the impact? In your workbook, **write** or **type** your responses.

Take your ideas and insights from above and try to **write/type** one inspiring Purpose.

If this is helpful, try using the framework that includes both the activity you do and the results you achieve (for example: "My purpose is to **activity with result(s)**," or, "My purpose is to **result through activity**"). Going back to my example, the "sharing knowledge and experience" is the activity, the "grow and succeed" is the result. Below are a few more examples:

My purpose is to help people solve problems to live a better life.

My purpose is to raise happy and healthy kids who make a positive difference in the world.

My purpose is to achieve economic freedom by becoming a sought-after expert in my field.

Finding Your STRENGTHS and Discovering Your SUPERPOWERS

Have you ever noticed that time flies when you're doing activities you enjoy, are good at, or that come naturally to you? Hours pass in what feels like minutes because you are doing something that utilizes your unique gifts and talents. You find you're operating at a deeper level, with more energy and enthusiasm, which **aligns with your Purpose** and leads to greater levels of achievement. This is what happens when you use the traits, skills, talents, and knowledge that make up your **Strengths**. This doesn't just benefit you. It also benefits the people you work or interact with. When you know your Strengths and apply them, you position yourself for more success as a leader of people, teams, and organizations.

In addition, research indicates that when we use our Strengths, we're happier, more engaged, more productive, better teammates, and we enjoy a greater quality of life in general.[1,2]

74%
more engaged when we have a chance to use our Strengths at work.

31%
more productive when we have awareness of our Strengths.

12%
more effective as a team when we know each other's Strengths.

3x
more likely to have excellent quality of life.

On the other hand, when we are forced to take on activities that don't align with our Strengths, it is often more difficult to muster up the energy, and procrastination becomes the reality. Not exactly a life being lived with Passion and Purpose.

Knowing your Strengths is critical in the discovery of who you are and positions you to achieve more clarity, focus, and success on your Great Life NOW journey. Let's dive into your Strengths.

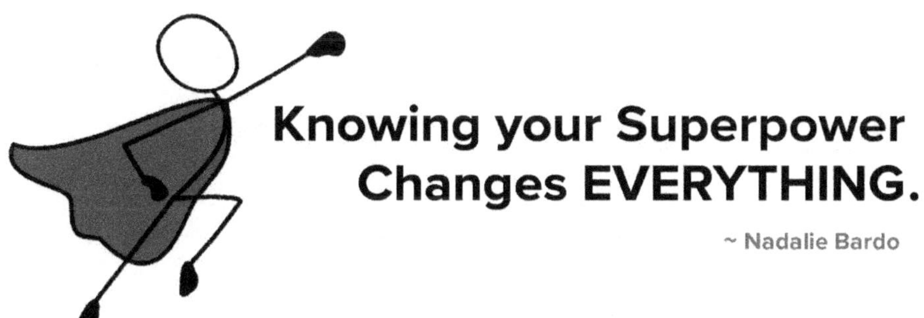

In your workbook . . .

Discovering Your Strengths and Superpowers

Your goal in this exercise is to get to your top two to three Strengths—your Superpowers that are unique to you and can help you succeed in life.

STEP 1 : Ask your people.

Don't take your word for it. Begin by finding out what your friends, teammates, or family think. Email at least three people and ask for their input.

Here's a sample script. Edit it however you like so it sounds as if it is coming from you.

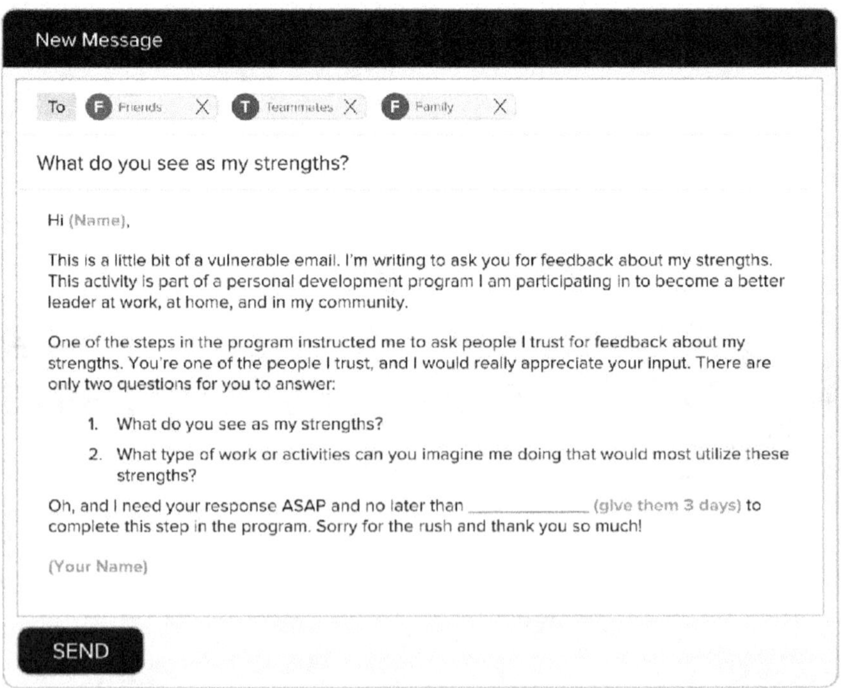

Hi (Name),

This is a little bit of a vulnerable email. I'm writing to ask you for feedback about my strengths. This activity is part of a personal development program I am participating in to become a better leader at work, at home, and in my community.

One of the steps in the program instructed me to ask people I trust for feedback about my strengths. You're one of the people I trust, and I would really appreciate your input. There are only two questions for you to answer:

1. What do you see as my strengths?
2. What type of work or activities can you imagine me doing that would most utilize these strengths?

Oh, and I need your response ASAP and no later than ______________ (give them 3 days) to complete this step in the program. Sorry for the rush and thank you so much!

(Your Name)

After you receive all the feedback, read through the responses to find themes. Use the space below to make a list of five to ten Strengths you've been told you have. Even if you don't agree that something is one of your Strengths, if you heard it from multiple people, write it down.

TOP STRENGTHS DISCOVERED

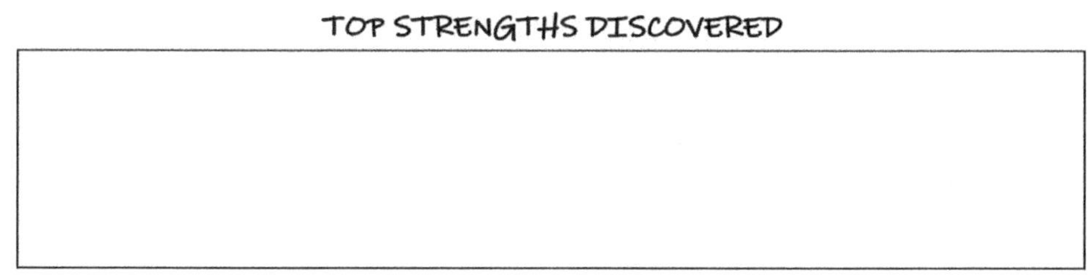

STEP 2 : Document who you are on your best day.

Now it's time for your perspective on your Strengths. Think of three separate experiences in your life when you were at your best. Use these prompts to help think of times when you:

- **Felt like you were in your element.**
- **Accomplished something important to you.**
- **Succeeded in doing something that made you proud.**
- **Felt you were put to good use.**
- **Overcame a big challenge.**
- **Felt yourself thriving, winning, or achieving something great.**
- **Led the way out of a crisis.**

For each experience, write about what you were doing. Think deeply to discover the Strengths you were using in that moment. Use the next page to **write (type)** the Strengths that you find.

Example:

Write about an experience of you at your best:
I remember the excitement and relief after stepping off the stage having delivered a keynote speech to more than 2,500 people. The feeling was exhilarating, yet also a huge sense of relief and pride for the work I put into crafting what turned out to be a 90-minute, one act play. I came up with some innovative ways to share the content and kept the audience engaged from the first sentence to the final close.

Strengths discovered:
Focused, creative thinking, confident, being persuasive, helping others get excited to take action.

Write about an experience of you at your best:

Strengths discovered:

Write about an experience of you at your best:

Strengths discovered:

Write about an experience of you at your best:

Strengths discovered:

STEP 3 : Dive deeper to discover more.

On the next page are four questions to help you dive deeper into your Strengths. These questions are designed to open your consciousness to something you may not have ever thought of before, even if it was staring you right in the face.

Think about your personal and professional experiences. It is important to consider as many aspects of your life as possible. And don't worry about repeating yourself. You may have similar responses to different questions. **Repetition simply validates that the Strength is core to who you are.**

DEEP DIVE QUESTIONS

What are you naturally good at? (You know, the things that come easily, that just feel second nature to you.)

What do you enjoy doing at work, that's not part of your job description, that you just take on without anyone asking you to?

What knowledge and skills have you developed that you find valuable?

What tends to be your role with friends and family?

STEP 4 : Find your Superpowers.

Reflect on everything you've discovered about your Passion, Purpose, and Strengths and use your intuition to determine your unique abilities. Refer back to your lists of Strengths provided by family, teammates, and friends, as well as your own lists uncovered in Steps 2 and 3.

Make a new list below. Group similar Strengths together to create themes. For instance, "relatable," "being outgoing," and "building relationships" could fall under one theme of "connecting with people." Or, "good with numbers" and "problem-solver" could fall under "being analytical."

Next, define your Superpowers. Your Superpowers should encompass your top two to three Strengths—the ones that you prioritized as the strongest.

1. ______________________________

2. ______________________________

3. ______________________________

Congratulations on discovering your top two to three Superpowers! You will soon see that leveraging these Strengths will help you to determine your values and the behaviors that bring those values to life. These Strengths will help you to make smart, confident choices about which areas of your life to most focus on improving.

By using these Strengths, you'll be doing more of what you are good at and ultimately will get more of what you want... which is a Great Life NOW with less stress and fear and more happiness and success.

Congratulations on discovering your Strengths and Superpowers.

Let's pause to consider your priorities.

Life and Two Cans of Beer

What follows is an old story with respect to priorities and focus. I didn't write it, I found it. It is one of those anecdotes that is worth reading and passing along. Please enjoy and take the spirit of this tale as you proceed into the next part of designing your Great Life NOW.

A professor stood before his philosophy class with some items in front of him.

When the class began, he said, "We all have this one life to live. A fleeting shadow against all that exists in this vast universe. We have the ability to accomplish anything. Truly anything. If we use our time wisely." He then put a large, empty pickle jar on the desk and, without a word, proceeded to fill it with golf balls.

He then asked the students if the jar was full. They agreed that it was.

So, the professor then picked up a box of pebbles and poured them into the jar. He shook the jar lightly, and the pebbles rolled into the open areas between the golf balls.

He again asked the students if the jar was full.

They agreed it was.

The professor picked up a box of sand and poured it into the jar. Of course, the sand filled up every remaining space.

He asked once more if the jar was full.

The students responded with a unanimous yes.

The professor then produced two cans of beer from under the table and poured the entire contents into the jar, effectively filling the empty spaces between the grains of sand.

The students laughed.

"Now," said the professor, as the laughter subsided, "I want you to recognize that this jar represents your life. **The golf balls are the important things**—your family, your children, your health, your friends, your favorite passions—things that if everything else was lost and only they remained, your life would still be full. **The pebbles are the other things that matter** like your job, your house, your car. **The sand is everything else**—the small stuff."

"If you put the sand into the jar first," he continued, "there is no room for the pebbles or the golf balls. The same goes for life. If you spend all your time and energy on the small stuff, you will never have room for the things that are important to you. Pay attention to the things that are critical to your happiness. Play with your children. Take time to get medical checkups. Take your partner out to dinner. Play another 18. There will always be time to clean the house and fix the disposal. **Take care of the golf balls first, the things that really matter. Set your priorities. The rest is just sand."**

One of the students raised his hand and inquired what the beer represented.

The professor smiled.

"I'm glad you asked," he said. "It just goes to show you that no matter how full your life may seem, there's always room for a couple of beers with friends."

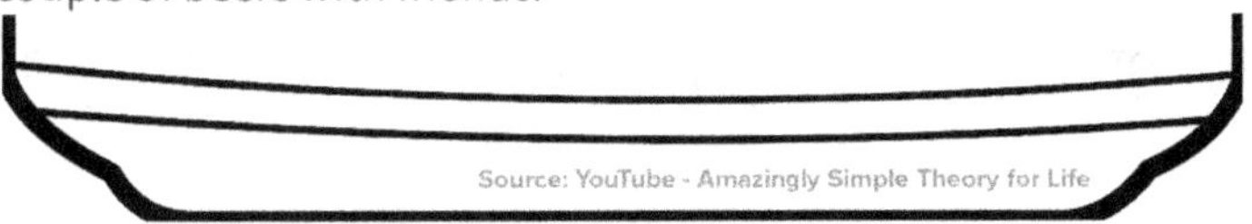

Source: YouTube - Amazingly Simple Theory for Life

(https://www.youtube.com/watch?v=uTkvEUwYfpY)[3]

Time for GRATITUDE

What is gratitude?

Gratitude is the greatest virtue of all, as it enables us to connect with something larger than ourselves, something profoundly good and comforting. Demonstrating gratitude opens your eyes to the miracles in life and positively influences your attitude, health, and relationships, leading to less stress and more optimism, enthusiasm, and joy while also enabling tranquility, empathy, and greater consciousness.

The opposite of expressing gratitude is to focus on what you lack or what other people have that you don't.

But this mindset leads to more stress, envy, and unhappiness—what the great motivational speaker and sales guru, Zig Ziglar, referred to as "stinkin' thinkin'." Not exactly the recipe for a Great Life NOW.

The reality is gratitude does not always come easily to humans, and it seems to be a diminishing virtue in our modern, consumerist society. It is often more natural to focus on what we don't have instead of appreciating what we do.

The amount of time you spend on gratitude each day will help influence how great your life is. Those living a Great Life NOW spend at least a few moments a day practicing gratitude. Doing so reveals a bigger and better perspective of life, where opportunity and possibilities are at the forefront.

On your next stop on the Great Life NOW journey, you will further develop your skillset of gratitude.

In your workbook . . .

Gratitude Check-In

Show yourself how easy it is to be grateful. Stop and view your life through the eyes of the other eight billion people on Earth. Is it not true that billions of them would gladly trade places with you right now? In fact, is it not true that most of them would be overjoyed to do so?

Jot down or **type** a few thoughts for each of the prompts below.

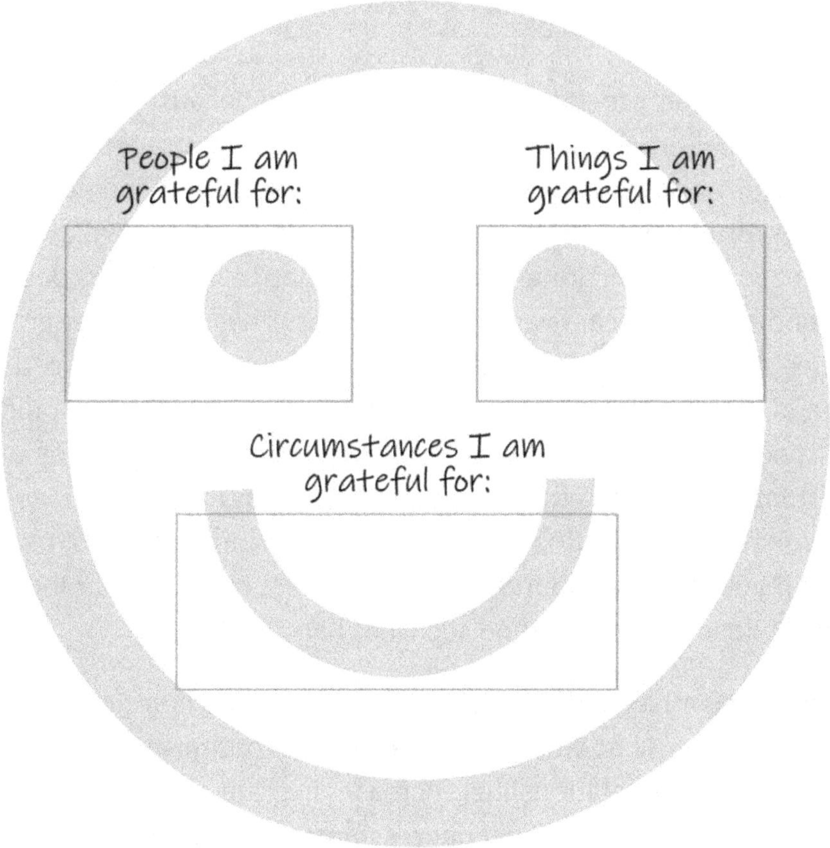

People I am grateful for:

Things I am grateful for:

Circumstances I am grateful for:

The Science of GRATITUDE

Gratitude can increase important neurochemicals that make us feel better. When our thinking shifts from negative to positive, there is a surge of feel-good chemicals such as dopamine, serotonin, and oxytocin in our brains. These all contribute to feelings of closeness, connection, and happiness.

Thanks to decades of scientific research, we know that gratitude also exerts a powerful influence over our social, physical, and mental health. That's right; gratitude will also make you a healthier human!

Socially, gratitude provides significant benefits because, after all, gratitude is a social emotion. Consider it a relationship-strengthening emotion; it requires us to see how we have been supported and accepted by others. Gratitude also helps bind us together with others. Behavioral scientists have used functional magnetic resonance imaging to determine how people experience a variety of emotions. They found that gratitude activates the brain regions that govern feelings of reward and the formation of social bonds. Researchers refer to it as the "find, remind, and bind" theory, and it proves that demonstrating gratitude helps us find "good quality" candidates for friends and mates as it helps "remind" us of the goodness of our existing relationships, and it further "binds" us to others. So, if you have not found that near-perfect mate yet, try increasing your daily dose of gratitude and see what happens!

Behavioral scientists have also proven that gratitude is critical to psychological well-being. In addition to increasing your optimism and happiness, and improving your relationships, increases in gratitude often lower stress and potentially even counteract depression and thoughts of hopelessness that can lead to suicide.

> **While gratitude is only one piece of the mental health puzzle, it is a mighty one.**

As more and more research is conducted in the field of gratitude, there are mixed results concerning its impact on **physical** health. A growing body of literature suggests that grateful people may have better sleep, healthier hearts, and fewer aches and pains. While the physical health benefits continue to be inconclusive, the social and mental health benefits remain quite clear.

By now, you realize that gratitude is much more than just positive thinking and appreciating what you have. It's also the key to decreasing the toxic "stinkin' thinkin'" that fuels negativity and leads to fewer friends, loneliness, and poor overall health.

So, gratitude has the potential to improve our lives socially, mentally, and physically all while helping us to downshift our negative thinking, so we can be more enjoyable people to be around for ourselves and everyone else. It sounds like we should all be more grateful, doesn't it?

Are you up for the challenge?
It's time for the 30-Day Gratitude Challenge.

In your workbook . . .

30-Day Gratitude Challenge

Given the extraordinary benefits that gratitude bestows on our brains and bodies, establishing a gratitude practice may be one of the least costly and most accessible forms of natural medicine that you have to tap into.

The gratitude exercises you will engage in for the next 30 days will help you to recognize the good in your own life, appreciate the goodness in others, and develop a stronger overall appreciation for the opportunities in your life, right NOW.

The magnitude of your own experience will depend on the effort you expend. So, dive in because you're about to participate in one of the most beneficial mental health practices that science has to offer.

Let's do this!

Exercise 1 – The Daily Dig to Find the Good

For 30 days, write down at least one thing you are grateful for. Start a journal, either online or on paper. Ask yourself some thought-starter questions. Below are a few to spark your thinking.

- What is in my life right now that is a blessing?
- What happened yesterday or today that I'm grateful for?
- Did I benefit in any way because of someone else's actions?
- What are the signs and signals the universe is sending me?

For best results, write with as much specificity as possible. Do not hesitate to write a few sentences that describe in detail what happened or what might happen that you would be grateful for.

You should do this exercise at whatever time works best for your schedule. Studies indicate that an evening practice promotes better and longer sleep. On the other hand, I've found that beginning my day with my gratitude practice gets me in the right mindset for creativity and taking action. Regardless of the time of day, what matters most is that you "do" the gratitude that will shift your mental state in ways that improve your life.

Exercise 2 – The Thankful Reframe

Think about a time in your life when you experienced a significant setback and reframe it to spark gratitude. You can write a few paragraphs or a few pages. What is critical is to conjure an event from your past when something didn't go the way you were hoping. Then reframe it to find the good. Maybe it was the worst day of your life when it happened, but now, with time and healing, you can see the positive consequences. Did you grow as a person? Did it open up deeper communication with loved ones? Did it give you perspective about your life's course?

Early on in my career, I came up with what I thought was the perfect business idea. The year was 2000, when most small businesses could not dream of affording a website for their business, not to mention the idea of selling their product or service online. Before the 2000's, the yellow pages were where people let their "fingers do the walking" as websites could only be afforded by large companies. I realize that for most of us, remembering a time when every business didn't at least have a website listing is quite distant in our memory. But in the year 2000, our tech-focused world had not yet reached a point where everyone had a friend, family member, or close acquaintance who could code a website, and website development had not evolved to the advanced state of today. Only a few businesses were developing websites, and the cost was upwards of $30,000 or more for a site where you could promote and sell your goods and services.

My business idea was to create a website hosting platform for small businesses that was a combination of the yellow pages and the Better Business Bureau, where users could rank providers by their experience. Whether you were looking for a dentist, photographer, mechanic, or lawyer, the Local Wizard was going to be the place to be. The Local Wizard was a name I came up with because I thought each geographic market would have its own "wizard" and associated domain name for shoppers.

At the time, Karyn and I had celebrated our first year of marriage and were expecting our first child. I was also finishing up my MBA from the Simon School at the University of Rochester. I was working day and night between school and crafting the blueprint of success for the Local Wizard.

My friend Patrick Ahern joined me in this endeavor. He helped put the finishing touches on the business plan, and we began recruiting a team of people that we thought could help develop the technology and sell the product. Together, we also began pitching to investors. The interest level was tremendous right out of the gate.

Tom, a billionaire investor, stepped forward, committing a few million dollars on our first meeting. Tom was the founder and CEO of a Fortune 1000 company that provided payroll services to small businesses. I'll never forget the moment we ended our first meeting together when Tom looked at Patrick and me and said, "Don't speak to any other investors; you've got all the money you need right here."

There were a few catches, though. First, Tom wanted us to change the name to Yelp. He "hated the yellow pages" because of the incredible investment he made buying advertisements to market his company in each city across the country. In his mind, they had a monopoly and charged way too much. He loved his idea of a name that sounded like them but was something completely different—something that could put them out of business.

At first, I was not too fond of the name Yelp as I had grown quite attached to the Local Wizard concept. However, I also didn't have any money, especially 2.5 million dollars, which as Patrick was quick to point out, was exactly what Tom committed to at our first meeting.

So, we changed the name from Local Wizard to Yelp. Yes, I was the first domain name holder of www.yelp.com back in the year 2000. Looking back now, I probably should not have let that one expire.

With our business plan intact and a small team of eager participants ready to join as full-time software developers and salespeople, we were ready to launch. All we needed to do was finalize the investment deal.

While sitting in a large conference room with Tom and our attorneys, a call came in that changed everything. Tom left the room and returned a few minutes later with a starry eyed, confused, and almost frightened look on his face. He had just heard the most terrible news about Gene, his best friend, who started the company with him. Gene had been diagnosed with stage IV pancreatic cancer. I learned later he was given only a few weeks to live.

The meeting wrapped up quickly, and we agreed to come together again in a few days. Two days later, I received a call from Tom, and it was not good news. "Gregg, I get at least one business plan a week on my desk from entrepreneurs who believe they have the next big idea. This one you brought to me is one of the best I've seen in years. However, I can't invest right now. With Gene's diagnosis, I've been reminded that I need to stay 100% focused on my company in the coming months."

When I hung up the phone, I was shocked. I felt great sorrow for Gene. But at the moment, I also found myself feeling sorry for myself. Whether right or wrong, I felt as if I'd just lost the best potential investor we could have had. As it turned out, Gene passed away within a few weeks. I didn't know him but heard he was a fantastic guy and appreciated Tom's incredible bond with him.

Patrick and I had to move on. It was time to revisit the conversations with many other investors we'd presented to before meeting Tom. Several had shown a strong desire to invest. However, we soon realized that was not about to happen either.

A few days later, on March 10th, 2000, the Nasdaq stock index began its bear market collapse. This was the day the "tech-bubble burst." The Nasdaq index had risen from 1,000 to more than 5,000 between the years of 1995 and 2000. The euphoria left us with plenty of investors looking for the next big tech thing. However, from the moment of March 10th, every investor we had spoken to was more than a little spooked. And they had every right to be. As it turned out, over the next few years, the Nasdaq plummeted more than 75%, leaving investors leery of all technology start-ups promising fast growth yet requiring large infusions of capital.

While we weren't a public company, investors' moods made raising capital for a technology company darn near impossible, especially for one that included a platform that had never been seen or heard of before.

In what felt like an instant, a business plan we'd worked on for a year went up in flames. I was relatively broke, had a newly minted MBA, a new home, new marriage, and a baby only a few months away. I had to do something to kickstart a career. But clearly, it was not going to be in the high-tech world. At least not yet.

I moved on and started Brand Integrity, which began as a culture consulting company. There I had the chance to work for nearly 20 years with amazing teammates and clients. Patrick joined me, and together we created something extraordinary. We brought together a team of great people who created culture-changing strategies and programs that greatly impacted our clients' success. Eventually, we got our "technology bug" satisfied by creating an employee engagement software that helped fuel Brand Integrity's growth. It's what led to the successful sale of the company. As I think back now, without having failed at our start-up endeavor, we never would have developed the relationships with teammates and clients we've made or had the impact we've had on so many people.

In 2003, I also began a teaching career at my alma matter, the Simon School at the University of Rochester, and kick-started the speaking and coaching careers I have today. Would any of this have happened if I didn't face the failed effort of Yelp? Maybe, but probably not.

Your past struggle may be minuscule in comparison to mine or might be much more life-altering. As long as it's an episode that sparked a change in course or left you feeling as if something was unresolved, then it's worth considering. Maybe it's something that still evokes a trace of uneasiness and discomfort. Perhaps it's a time your heart was broken, or you were bypassed for a promotion. Maybe it was a time you behaved poorly or betrayed a family member or friend. How did the experience open the door for you to become an even better human or lead to even better opportunities? Did the event help you meet your current spouse or lead you down your current career path? Can you see how your current life situation turned out better than you thought it would at the time?

When you sit down to write, give yourself a private, comfortable space, free of distractions. Think intently about the past and trace a line from the setback you experienced to the good that ultimately resulted.

You are not being asked to pretend that something is better when it is not. Instead, seek out an adverse event and explore the positives resulting from how you responded and what it led to.

These first two exercises were designed to help you find the good in your life. This next exercise will turn your attention outward to honor the people who've made a difference in your life. You'll have the opportunity to share your joy.

Exercise 3 – The Personal Touch

Over the next 30 days, you will leverage the power of the personal touch to share gratitude and joy with those in your life who deserve your thanks.

There are two parts to this exercise.

Part 1 – The Handwritten Note

Over the next 30 days, write five Appreciation Cards and send them to people who deserve your gratitude. It may be tempting to send an email instead. Don't! Just think about the last time you received a thank-you email. It probably arrived while you were busy with work or rushing to a meeting or out the door. It's likely the sender's sentiments were appreciated but quickly forgotten.

Next, imagine the recipient of your Appreciation Card going to their mailbox and finding your handwritten note. What feelings might it invoke? Will they appreciate your effort more so than if you merely hit "send" on an email?

Begin by thinking of someone who provided help that changed your life in some way, then write a few sentences to honor them:

1. **Reflect** on what they did for you or gave you.
2. **Recognize** the goodness of the deed or gift and of the giver.
3. **Thank** them for their help or kindness.

It's not enough to say, "Thanks for ________." Instead, tell them what they did that had an impact on your life. For example, *When I was home sick with the flu, you regularly checked in on how I was doing and made me feel loved. Thanks for being such a good friend.* Or, *When I was running behind at work, you stepped up to help me with carpooling the kids. That was awesome and really helped me. I am so grateful for your friendship.*

Expressing gratitude takes only a few minutes out of your day, but the impact can last a lifetime. You'll be spreading positivity while strengthening personal and professional relationships.

Do it. It will feel good.

Aiden,

When I was home sick with the flu, you regularly checked in on how I was doing and made me feel loved. Thanks for being such a good friend.

Your Friend,

Gregg

Heidi,

When I was running behind at work, you stepped up to help me with carpooling the kids. That was awesome and really helped me.

I am so grateful for your friendship.

I appreciate you,

Gregg

Part 2 – The Handwritten Letter (and Visit) Experience

Think about someone who has provided you with guidance, gifts, or inspiration that has positively impacted your life. Are there friends or family members who took a special interest in your well-being? Is there a coworker who has helped you along the way? A coach or teacher who pushed you to be your best? Is there someone in your life who, if they were gone tomorrow, you'd regret that you hadn't thanked them? This may be the perfect person for you to begin the Handwritten Letter Experience with.

Write them a letter of thanks for who they are and what they've done to impact your life. Specifically describe the time, place, feelings, and results of their efforts. Be as descriptive as possible.

Next, schedule a visit with the person you are honoring and read them the letter out loud. Then leave the letter with them so they can enjoy it forever.

That's it. It's that easy. Write a letter. Read it to them. And then enjoy the immeasurable benefits that both of you will reap from this experience that you created and delivered.

You possess an unlimited capacity to feel and express gratitude. Your ability to find the good and share the joy is truly endless. As you triumph through your 30-Day Gratitude Challenge, you'll move from a state of gratitude to the trait of gratitude. This will lead to the social, mental, and physical health benefits which will provide you the fuel to continue this valuable practice. Keep finding the good and sharing the joy with others, and the rewards will be tenfold for a better life… a Great Life NOW.

The Brand Called YOU

You get to make up the rules.

As stated earlier, life is a game like all other games. The only difference is many people don't realize they are playing. They go through the motions where some days they win and some days they feel like they're losing. Sadly, some feel like they are losing more than winning.

When you are living a Great Life NOW, you are winning consistently. Why? Because, like any game, there are rules, and... YOU GET TO MAKE UP THE RULES!

Your values are the rules by which the game of life is played. Identifying your values is a deeply personal exercise about uncovering what is most important to you. Your values are the sacred guidelines that, when followed, bring immense satisfaction and meaning to your life.

Your core values are a representation of your self-worth, and they are the most important piece of knowledge you can own. Consider them your ticket to a great life.

Your values power The Brand Called YOU.

Everyone has values. They exist for you and every human being regardless of whether you recognize them. Your values should align with your Purpose, leverage your Strengths and Superpowers, and come to life in how you think, speak, and act. How you live your values affects your self-worth and ultimately, your reputation among family, friends, colleagues, and anyone else you interact with. This is your brand—The Brand Called YOU.

Your values are what you believe to be important to the way you live and work. Those who consistently act out of alignment with their values are not experiencing a Great Life NOW as they likely feel drained and stressed, which can be a real source of unhappiness.

How do you know if you are living your brand?

When you honestly define your values, state them as the rules of the game, and then play by those rules, you are truly living your brand and living an evolved lifestyle. From this point forward, consider your Great Life NOW journey as a lifestyle that is powered by the core of who you are: your values, your rules, your brand.

In the exercise that follows, you will have an opportunity to define the rules you will play by.

When you
honestly
define
your
values,
state them
as the rules
of the game,
and then
play by those rules,
you are
truly living
your brand
and living a Great Life.

EXERCISE

In your workbook . . .

The Brand Called YOU—Your Core Values

STEP 1 : Warm up.

To get your mind focused on values-based thoughts, **jot down** or **type** answers to the following questions.

What are the three things you like most about yourself?

Who are the two people you like and respect the most and why?

STEP 2 : List the top 10 potential values to power your brand.

Highlight key words from Step 1 that reflect what you feel is important in your life. Then, review the table of examples to further spark your thinking around values you want to be known for. Make note of the key words that speak to you. Feel free to combine or create new ones.

Sample Words to Consider

(Words that could be part of your set of values. Use them to spark your thinking.)

Accountability
Accuracy
Achievement
Advancement
Adventure
Altruism
Ambition
Assertiveness
Authenticity
Balance
Being the best
Belonging
Boldness
Calmness
Carefulness
Challenge
Cheerfulness
Collaboration
Commitment
Community
Compassion
Competitiveness
Connectedness
Courage
Creativity
Curiosity
Decisiveness
Dedication
Discipline
Diversity
Effectiveness
Efficiency
Elegance
Empathy
Empowerment
Enjoyment
Enlightenment
Enthusiasm
Entrepreneurship
Equality
Ethical
Excellence
Excitement
Expertise
Faith
Fame
Family
Fitness
Flexibility
Focus
Forgiveness
Freedom
Friendship
Fun
Goodness
Gratitude
Greatness
Growth
Happiness
Harmony
Healing
Health
Helping society
Home
Honesty
Humility
Humor
Improvement
Independence
Individuality
Influence
Ingenuity
Innovation
Inquisitiveness
Insightfulness
Integrity
Intelligence
Intuition
Involvement
Joy
Justice
Kindness
Knowledge
Leadership
Learning
Life
Love
Loyalty
Making a difference
Mastery
Money
Nature
Nirvana
Openness
Order
Originality
Partnership
Passion
Patience
Peace
Perfection
Perseverance
Personal development
Philanthropy
Pleasure
Power
Privacy
Productivity
Professionalism
Purpose
Quality
Relationship
Respect
Responsibility
Responsiveness
Safety
Scrutiny
Self-esteem
Serenity
Service
Sharing
Simplicity
Spirituality
Stability
Status
Stewardship
Strength
Success
Teamwork
Tradition
Trust
Truth
Understanding
Uniqueness
Variety
Vitality
Wealth
Wellness
Winning
Wisdom
Work

Next, **write** or **type** up to 10 potential values that make up who you are and what you want to be known for. These will be the leading candidates for your "rules to live by"—the rules that will power The Brand Called YOU.

STEP 3 : Define The Brand Called YOU — WHO YOU ARE.

The Brand Called YOU represents your most important Core Values. This is arguably the most difficult part of the exercise where you must make choices on the highest priority Core Values for your future. In addition to the candidates above, consider your work to date, including:

- What makes you happy
- What you fear
- Your Purpose
- Your Superpowers

Taking all of this into consideration, what are the top Core Values that, when you live them consistently, will lead to a Great Life NOW?

EXAMPLES:

- Strong Relationships
- Being Healthy
- Learn & Grow

List each value and explain in a few sentences why "living it" every day is important to you.

My Core Values:	Why they are important:

Your values are your rules for the game of life.

WARNING: Playing the game requires balance.

As you move forward with your Great Life NOW Game Plan, you are positioned to use your Core Values to evaluate important areas of growth and identify the goals and habits that keep you on a path to living a great life. This is an admirable situation since those values have been selectively chosen by you to be the perfect representation of you, on your best day, living your brand.

But, what do you do when you run into a conflict with your values? This will happen. You will experience situations where it appears that in order to live one value, you must sacrifice another. Oh no! What do you do?

We face these situations more often than you would think. Last year, I had to call one of my MBA students to discuss his “over the top” class participation. This individual spoke up too much in class—sometimes a dozen or more times in a two-hour lecture that included many students, all of whom were paying customers. When one person (or a few) dominates the time allotted for class participation, then naturally, frustration ensues. It was early in the semester, and I knew I needed to address this situation. And I understood I needed to let my values be my guide.

One of my Core Values is **Integrity Without Compromise**, which means being straightforward and honest in my communications. I have another value of **Kindness**. Both values play a daily role in guiding how I think and act. Sometimes, however, they are in conflict as they were when I had to call this student. The Kindness side of me wanted to shower him with accolades because I assumed he was a very good student and could tell he was quite smart, yet the Integrity Without Compromise value overruled here and I let him know (in as nice a way as possible) that he was speaking up way too much in class. I shared that in our last class, he spoke up to express his opinion more than 10 times. Of course, he was surprised. I also shared my perspective, asking him to imagine if everyone spoke up even half as much as he did. That would lead to hundreds of opinions being shared, not leaving much time for the lecture or the planned learning activities. In this instance, my Integrity Without Compromise value outweighed my Core Value of Kindness. However, that's not always the case.

Yesterday, my wife Karyn asked whether I liked her new shoes. I really didn't like them all that much. In fact, they looked quite uncomfortable, and I had an idea that they were very expensive. Uncomfortable and expensive don't go well together for me. Still, I wasn't born yesterday and have been married for nearly 25 years, so I knew that my Core Value of Kindness needed to be the "rule to live by" in this particular moment.

I share these examples to make the point that we live in a perfectly imperfect world where sometimes we must do a little balancing of our values. Not because we are being disingenuous or misleading, but because we are human. Sometimes your values will conflict, and, in that case, you'll need to determine which one should be the priority in guiding how you think, what you say, and how you act. This does not mean you are not acting with integrity. Quite the opposite in fact. When you take the time to think about what you value and allow it to guide how you think, speak, and act, you are demonstrating significant integrity with respect to The Brand Called YOU!

Living The Brand Called YOU

Imagine you are walking alone down the street and you come across a scrappy-looking coyote. What are your first impressions of the animal? Does it seem ferocious? Threatening? Conniving? Scary? Fast? Your answer is most likely a yes to all of these. Why? Because you've watched animal documentaries or movies depicting how coyotes behave. You see animals in action and form impressions. This is how you know to trust a Labrador Retriever more than a crocodile. By watching them, a "brand" is formed in your mind.

Humans are no different than other creatures in the animal kingdom. We watch each other and form our opinions. This means you can have the most elegantly stated Core Values, but if you don't know how to act them out—or worse, you act in ways that are counter productive to those values—then guess what? That is your brand. Your reputation.

Keep this in mind: People will judge you by the experience they have or that someone they know has when interacting with you.

She remembered who she was and the game changed.

-Lalah Delia

One way to think about this is that your Core Values, regardless of how special they are to you, are completely invisible until you make them visible. In the simplest form, you can't say one of your Core Values is Being Friendly if you don't smile and say hello to people. Because it's invisible. So, that is what you will do in this next exercise—make the invisible visible.

You can't
talk your way out
of something you
behaved your way into.
You must
behave your way out.

In your workbook . . .

Make the Invisible Visible

In this exercise, you will have the opportunity to explore ideal behaviors that bring your Core Values to life, as well as actions you do that sometimes cause you to be out of alignment with your values.

STEP 1 : List Continue, Stop, Start activities.

On your best day, how do you demonstrate your values? (What should you **CONTINUE** doing?)	What things do you do that are out of alignment with your values? (What should you **STOP** doing?)	What can you begin doing or do more consistently to bring your values to life? (You guessed it … what should you **START** doing?)
CONTINUE	**STOP**	**START**

Need some help thinking of behaviors? Use these example behaviors to spark your thinking. Pick any that align with your values or simply review them to get an idea of how to write a specific behavior.

- Listen carefully to the ideas and opinions of others.
- Invest time to reflect, be grateful, and quiet the mind.
- Demonstrate genuine care and concern.
- Read at least one new book each month.
- Ensure employees have the knowledge and resources to do their jobs.
- Call __________ just to say hi.
- Accept others without judgment.
- Communicate clearly, effectively, and in a timely manner.
- Show up on time.
- Acknowledge mistakes and take proactive steps to improve.
- Appreciate and recognize others.
- Help people feel respected and understand the difference they make.
- Help others learn and grow.
- Effectively address difficult issues in a timely manner.
- Encourage and empower employees to take action.
- Say or do something nice for _____ every day.
- Speak positively about others.
- Proactively discuss when expectations have not been met.
- Use data to confirm progress and areas for improvement.
- Strengthen relationship(s) with _______.

STEP 2 : Document your behaviors.

Next, use the space below to summarize at least 10 behaviors you will focus on in both your personal and professional life. These should be specific actions you will commit to doing consistently that bring The Brand Called YOU to life.

Write/type your Core Value and list some behaviors underneath it. Behaviors should be directly aligned to the value they most represent. Do this for each of your Core Values.

Core Values and Behaviors

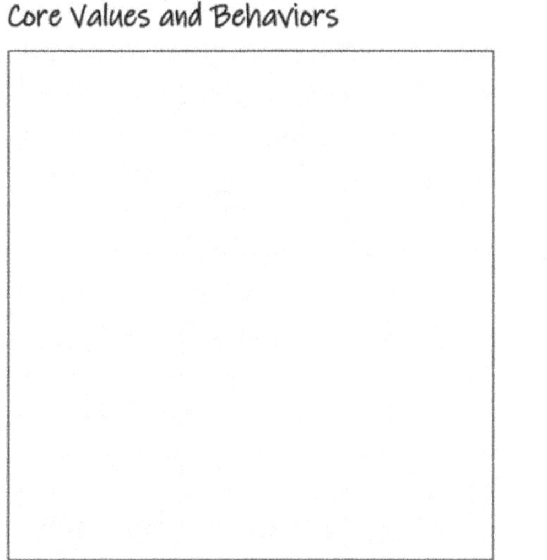

EXAMPLE:

Strong Relationships

- Reach out to friends, old and new, to reconnect and hear about their lives.
- Give more than I take.
- Notice and show appreciation for the successes of others.

Being Healthy

- Exercise five days a week.
- Eat healthier, smaller portions.
- Invest time daily to reflect, refocus, and quiet the mind.

Learn and Grow

- Read one educational book a month.
- Try new activities.
- Listen more than I talk.

STEP 3 : Rate how consistently you live it.

After you've carefully scripted each behavior in Step 2, go back and rate how consistently you currently live your brand. How consistently are you following your rules?

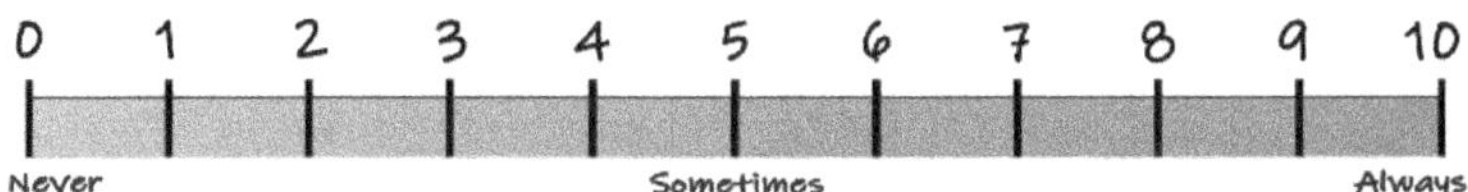

The Values Match

Now that you've got your rules in place (The Brand Called YOU) and know the optimal behaviors to bring your values to life, consider how well aligned you are with your employer. Whether self-employed or working for an organization, think about whether you have a "Values Match" where your values are aligned.

A strong work culture will have a belief system about what success looks like. Much like a human, an organization has a personality made up of beliefs and behavioral norms. If you are fortunate enough to work for a company with a strong, desirable work culture, you've probably noticed the existence of beliefs and behaviors that guide the organization's success. Good leaders know it is challenging to provide a culture that attracts and retains engaged employees and leads to consistently good, if not great, customer experiences without a strong set of cultural norms. Those norms make up the organization's brand and values—the rules of engagement.

How well do you match up? In the following exercise, jot down your Core Values and those of the organization where you work. How similar are they? In what ways are they different? How might you need to alter your beliefs and behaviors to excel at your job?

In your workbook . . .

Values Match

Connect the values that are aligned. Which ones are not aligned? Does it matter? If so, why?

The Brand Called YOU Your **VALUES**, Your **RULES**	**Your Organization's Brand** The **CORE VALUES**
______________________	______________________
______________________	______________________
______________________	______________________
______________________	______________________

How similar are they?

In what ways are they different?

How might you need to alter your beliefs and behaviors to excel at your job?

Your Mountains for GROWTH

To make sure you're living a Great Life NOW, you'll want to get laser-focused on the areas in your life where you have the best opportunities to grow. Remember what Coach Bob said when he helped me define my Purpose: "Where your focus goes, your energy will flow." This game of life is your game; you make the rules on how you want to live it and you get to design the areas where you want to focus your time, energy, and talents to ensure growth, personally and professionally.

Recall my mom's words of wisdom:

**"Once you have self-worth,
you can move mountains."**

It's time to discover what those mountains look like for you and get you moving forward.

What are the areas of your life where you want to grow?

So far, you've created your Pathway of Life, documented your Purpose and Superpowers, practiced the skill of gratitude, and defined your Core Values as The Brand Called YOU. Now it's time to take a deep dive into key areas of your life and ask a couple important questions:

Where are you doing well? And where are you struggling?

In the next exercise, you will determine the most important areas to focus on for growth in your Great Life NOW Game Plan.

The Great Life NOW Mountains for Growth™

No matter how accomplished or happy you are, you most likely have areas of your life that could use some improvement—and in many cases, different amounts of improvement.

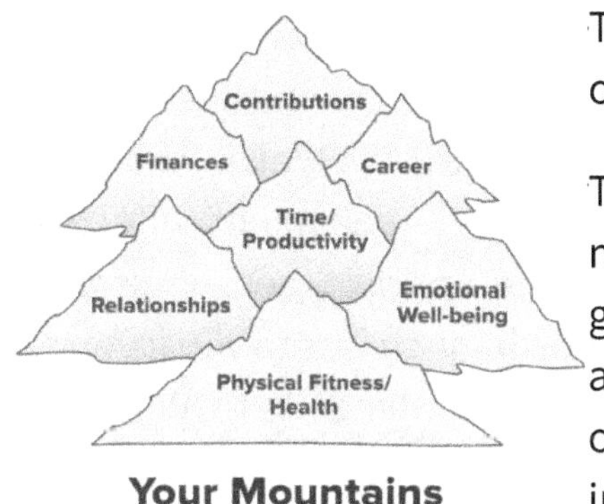

Your Mountains for GROWTH

There are seven areas for you to focus on. They are your Mountains for Growth.

The progress you make "moving your mountains" (i.e., moving forward in each growth area) will help create a more balanced life and fuel the Great Life NOW outcomes you desire: less stress, increased optimism, and more happiness and success. Each mountain has an impact on the others. When you struggle in one area, it can cause suffering in another.

Consider the example of your physical health. Have you reached the peak of your mountain with respect to physical fitness, feeling energetic and full of vitality? If not, consider the impact this has on your emotional well-being or productivity. It may be difficult to move your emotional mountain if you are consistently suffering physically.

If you've reached the mountain peak for physical fitness and health, congratulations! But now move on to another area. Are you highly satisfied with your relationships with family and friends? How about your finances? Are you on the right track to achieve financial freedom? What about your career? Does your job feel like a JOB, that is, something you go to every day to earn income, or is it more of a mission, something you enjoy going to because you feel respected and feel as if you made a positive impact on the lives of others?

The Great Life NOW Mountains for Growth is a simple, easy, and effective way to look at seven main areas of your life and rate how well you are doing so you can decide which mountains you should most focus on for improvement. When evaluating each area, consider your Core Values, your Purpose, and the Strengths and Superpowers you can bring to life.

While all seven mountains are important, there is a hierarchy that leads to a level of success and happiness that translates into a Great Life NOW. For example, if you don't master your **Physical Fitness/Health**, then your capacity to maximize your energy is compromised—you might suffer from chronic illness or die early. All the money in the world, career success, and contributions to your community will be worth much less to you if you are not here to enjoy them. You cannot experience a Great Life NOW without the vehicle that will help get you there.

Or, if you spend all your energy and time trying to solve your relationship problems, but are not optimizing your **Emotional Well-being**, you will always be at the mercy of life's challenges. Having a firm handle on your emotions, feeling as if you are in control of the chatter in your mind, frees you to be proactive rather than reactive to challenges and opportunities as they arise.

At the same time, it doesn't make sense to put all your energy and focus into your financial success while shortchanging **Relationships**. What is the point of becoming rich if you end up with a fractured family and very few friends?

Similarly, once you've improved how to **Productively Spend Your Time**, you increase your chances of **Career** success. Once you've made progress to improve your career, you can enhance the chances of growing your **Finances** and improve your ability to give back time and money (**Contributions**) to the people and causes that are most important to you.

This does not mean that you can't work on your finances and improving your health at the same time. Rather, it shows the importance and hierarchy of the Mountains for Growth—the seven areas to focus on to achieve a Great Life NOW.

"We all have two choices:
we can make a living
or we can design a life."

-Jim Rohn

In your workbook . . .

Your Mountains for Growth™

The objective of this exercise is to examine where you are now within each Mountain for Growth in order to determine the focus areas that will take you where you want to be.

STEP 1 : *Uncover where you are now.*

On a scale of 0 to 10, rate yourself based on where you are today. Be sure to consider the entire rating scale where 10 is completely satisfied, 5 is somewhat satisfied, and 0 means completely unsatisfied. Please do not compare yourself to others; this is about how satisfied you are with yourself in each of the seven areas.

After each rating, reflect on and write down why you gave yourself that score. What factors did you take into consideration?

Check the box that represents where you are now.

	0	1	2	3	4	5	6	7	8	9	10
Physical Fitness/Health											
Emotional Well-being											
Relationships											
Time/Productivity											
Career											
Finances											
Contributions											

Physical Fitness/Health — Where are you now and why?

Emotional Well-being — Where are you now and why?

Relationships — Where are you now and why?

Time/Productivity — Where are you now and why?

Career — Where are you now and why?

Finances — Where are you now and why?

Contributions — Where are you now and why?

STEP 2 : Document where you want to be.

For each Mountain for Growth, answer the following:

1. What is a reasonable score that would make you feel great? Describe in detail what it would look like to achieve your desired score.
2. Now that you've described what it looks like, document why improving is important. How will it affect your success in the other areas? What are the consequences if you don't improve?
3. Finally, describe what success could look like in the future. What are the key actions you could take toward that success?

Physical Fitness/Health

Emotional Well-being

Relationships

Time/Productivity

Career

Finances

Contributions

If, during this exercise, you discovered a unique mountain that will be important for your growth, add it below. Maybe you have a unique situation that calls for special attention, energy, and focus yet doesn't fit nicely into one of the seven prescribed mountains above. If so, use the space that follows to add it and follow the directions. Steps 1 and 2 outline where you are and where you want to be and what it will take to get there.

My Unique Mountain

You've come a long way in your Great Life NOW journey. At each step you've been thoughtful in evaluating your life, sparking ideas for the future, and planting seeds for ideal actions to take that will leverage your Strengths, bring your Purpose to life, and enable you to truly live The Brand Called YOU—all while moving forward in each of your Mountains for Growth. In the third and final part of the Great Life NOW journey, you will have the opportunity to determine what it will take to Activate your Game Plan.

The Universe Rewards Attitude and Action

3

ACTIVATING

ACTIVATING

To implement your Great Life NOW Game Plan requires activation of the right mindset, goals, and habits that will positively impact your Mountains for Growth and lead to more success over time. As you embark on activating your Game Plan, you can go down one of two pathways that are highlighted in the Great Life NOW Activation Curves™.

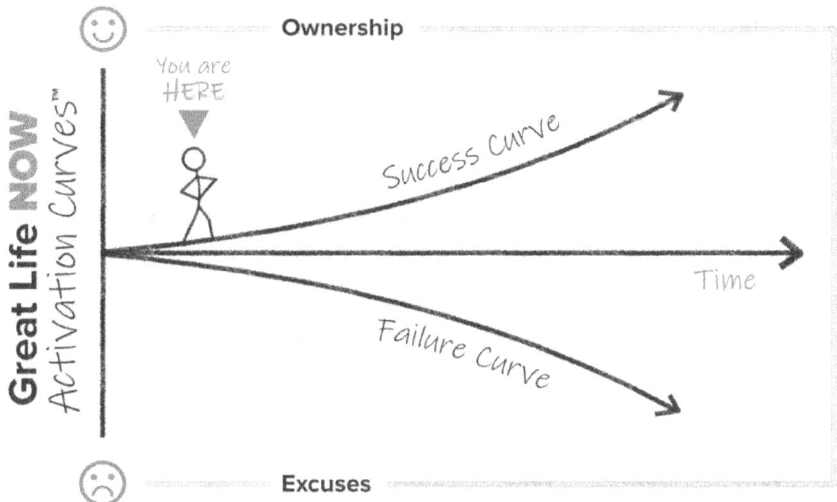

Those on the Success Curve have a mindset of ownership and remain focused and disciplined, while the dominant mindset for those on the Failure Curve is housed in excuses for why they could not make the continued investment.

Those on the Success Curve act based on a mantra I learned from my mentor and business partner, Tim Vottis: "If it's to be, it's up to me." They appreciate and have gratitude for all the people and circumstances that brought them to this point in their lives—their family, friends, teachers, and opportunities. But at the end of the day, they know they must "own" their brand and the beliefs, goals, and habits that lead to success. And that is how they achieve A Great Life NOW!

Stop and ask yourself: For each of your Mountains for Growth, will you be on the Success Curve, making progress by taking ownership, or will you be on the Failure Curve, making excuses and blaming other people and factors for why you didn't improve?

Life is like riding a bicycle… you are either moving forward, improving in your areas of focus, or standing still and falling off. This game of life you are designing is a game of motion fueled by emotion. You either experience positive motion on the Success Curve or a lack of motion on the Failure Curve. If you are not improving, enriching, and creating, then you are either running in place or worse, stepping backward as a human.

If you find yourself on the Failure Curve (and we all do at times), you don't have to stay there. Now is the time to take action to activate your Great Life NOW Game Plan by taking control of your mindset and building the beliefs, goals, and habits to grow and achieve success in each Mountain for Growth.

The only thing that can get in your way is YOU!

The Power of MINDSET and BELIEFS

A few years ago, I had the opportunity to share the stage at a conference with legendary author and motivational speaker Brian Tracy. Brian spoke just before me (no, he was not my opening act) and wowed the audience as he has done for more than four decades. Tough act to follow indeed. In his talk, he asked the audience to think about this question:

"What is the one thing you have complete control over in your life?"

Dead silence filled the room as hundreds of business leaders sat and wondered. His answer: "What you think about."

Brian proceeded to explain what everyone was very quickly catching on to: the idea that everything seems to be happening around us all day long, and much of it is truly beyond our control, except what we think about. In other words, he was saying we control our mindset, our way of thinking, our opinions. These opinions power our beliefs, which have a tremendous influence on how we act and how we interact with the people and the world around us.

Before we move on… take a moment to really think about this. What else can you control every minute of every day? Nothing.

> "The greatest discovery of my generation is that a human being can alter his life by altering his attitudes of mind."
>
> -William James
>
> (American philosopher, 1842-1910)

This is great news! Because if you want to change your life in any way, you first need to change your thinking. How quickly you change your mindset is up to you. But I will not sugarcoat it. Changing your mindset is not instant, and it's not as simple as "think happy thoughts and your problems miraculously go away." It takes a small amount of effort to get going and a large amount of discipline to keep going with the right mindset.

Choose a POSITIVE mindset.

You get to choose whether you will respond to life's situations and opportunities with an optimistic outlook and a positive, can-do attitude, or with a pessimistic outlook and a negative, what's-the-use attitude. The choice is yours. But make no mistake, your choice will land you on either the Success Curve or the Failure Curve when it comes to managing expectations, moving your mountains forward, and making meaningful progress in your life.

To raise your expectations for yourself, you have to get rid of all the excuses for why something *can't* be done and focus your thoughts on all the reasons it *can* and *will* be done.

This is where positive thinking comes in. And while it might seem like an easy choice, it is often more difficult to get across to people than you might imagine.

When I share this concept with my clients, some inevitably will chime in to say, "That's not being realistic." Yet, when I question that person about what is more realistic about a negative mindset, they can't answer me. This has happened to me countless times. I find the automatic assumption that negative thinking is more realistic than positive thinking to be pure lunacy. And you should too. Allow me to explain.

Study after study has proven that positive thinking leads to positive outcomes in life. Positive and optimistic people live longer, live healthier, have more energy, have more success in their careers, make better decisions, are more productive, are less stressed, and—not surprisingly—have healthier relationships and are much happier than negative people. And guess what? It is my opinion, and I imagine it might be yours too, that positive people are way more fun to be around.

Let's dive deep into why you think and feel the way you do.

In the next few sections, we will take a much deeper dive into why we think and emote the way we do. I'll apologize now if I offend you, as I'm going to take the liberty of making a few assumptions based on my experience working with humans over the past few decades. In most cases, these high-functioning individuals have set up "thinking systems" that keep people charging down the Failure Curve, making it difficult to consistently win in this game of life. If you are not one of those people who has set up a challenging thinking system so that you can't win, then again, I apologize in advance for my assumptions. Either way, please keep an open mind so that you can optimize your ability to stay on the Success Curve.

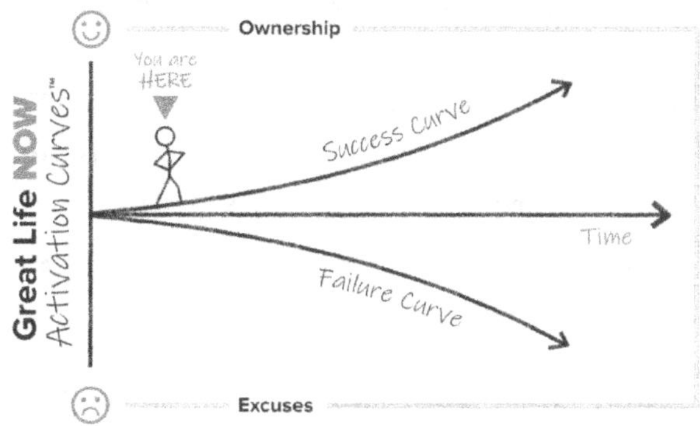

You are not your mind.

You are not your mind. You are the witness of your thoughts, which happen in your mind. Stay with me here, as this will all make perfect sense in a few moments.

You are a human who's been given this incredible gift of life. Life enters your mind each day through experiences that are stimulated by your senses. Whether taste, smell, hearing, touching, or seeing, these experiences enter your mind, where they are decrypted to create meaning or stuffed away to help protect you from thoughts and feelings that you won't like.

Each week, day, and hour, "life" is coming at you fast and furious, and you are in charge of controlling three things that most impact the way you think and act.

1. **The outside world.** It consists of everything that life offers through your five senses. You are conscious of what comes in, and it either feels nice to you or not so nice.

2. **Thoughts in your mind.** They are generated with or without you knowing.

3. **Emotions you feel.** When your thoughts are nice ones, you are living a Great Life. When they are not so nice, life is more difficult.

The difference between thoughts and emotions is important. If I asked you where your thoughts come from, you'd point to your head. That is because you intuitively know that thoughts come from your mind. They are verbal experiences that happen in your head. Your mind talks to you and often seems like a real voice, doesn't it?

You may talk to your mind, but you are not your mind. Instead, you are the witness of it. This is a very important point that I will come back to again.

**You are not your mind,
you are the witness of your mind.**

There are two types of thoughts: those you create and those your mind creates without you. We often refer to those thoughts created without our knowing as the "inner voice," and we all have it. In fact, researchers have proven that nearly 95% of your thoughts are created by your mind, not by you.[1] Again, you are just the witness to these thoughts. And unfortunately, in many cases, these thoughts are destructive, negative thoughts.

Of course, you do have a tremendous power within to create your own thoughts. But, as I will get to shortly, most people don't invest enough time and energy to do this.

If I asked you to think about a car, you could instantly do so. You can create an immediate visualization. It's as if you've got this gift, a mind that can think about what you tell it to think about.

If I asked you where your emotions come from, it might be a little less clear. You certainly wouldn't point to your head. When you tell someone you love them, you don't reference your head, you reference your heart. I am not referring to your physical heart, more so the energy that flows through your body, pumped by the heart. Emotions are felt, but you can't see them any more than you can see someone's thoughts. Your emotions are a vibration that gives off a sensation, an inner feeling that is often unrecognizable unless it becomes extreme. It's those extreme emotions that catch our attention. We will get to what causes those in just a few moments.

What I am trying to do here is teach you how to be the observer of YOU. Michael Singer, in his book *The Untethered Soul*, calls it the "seat of self," where your thoughts and emotions can and will change, yet you can be the witness of those changes.[2] In essence, you become aware of what is going on inside of you.

So, your mind and your heart are not you. But you have a clear view to look into your heart and mind. This is the essential message for you to take away. You are the witness. That is your role.

Your mind is the world's greatest device.

Your mind is like a computer, tablet, TV, or any other high-tech device that requires programming and an outside signal to optimize its usage. Its primary function is to receive a signal (an experience) from the outside world and then create a thought.

I like to think of the mind as a field of energy where our thoughts take place. An empty arena until we fill it up with life's daily experiences. These thoughts are invisible to everyone but you, which is why people can't yet read your mind. To be honest, I don't want to be here when they figure out how to read minds as that could get me (and you) in all kinds of trouble. Next thing you know, they'll create the "thought police" checking in on what we are thinking.

The ME Channel.

Your psyche is analogous to the program you are watching in your mind. Just like a program you'd watch on your devices, such as Netflix, Disney, or HBO, you have your channel. Just think, Howard Stern has his channel, so do Oprah (OWN) and The Beatles. You have the ME Channel that only talks to you and about you. It talks about what happened before, what you wish would happen next, and how you should feel about both.

We humans often try to change the channel, but guess who keeps showing up? YOU!

You get divorced, leave your job, find a new partner, get a new job, move to a new geographic location, and then the same things keep happening. Your challenges follow you like a shadow. Why?

Because you tried to change the channel, but there is only one channel, and it keeps playing all day long. What you need to change is you, your psyche that powers how you think, feel, speak, and act.

Psyche is a Greek term that means "the soul, mind, or spirit which occupies the physical body." The combination of your thoughts and emotions makes up your unique psyche. It's the show you are watching on your ME Channel, sometimes consciously but often unconsciously.

Your psyche will have a significant impact on your ability to move your mountains. Let's say you've struggled with relationships. Like most, you've struggled because of past experiences that have caused you to create thoughts and emotions about relationships. So, when life and the people in it don't jive just right with those thoughts and emotions, then you feel bad. What do you do then? You unconsciously act in ways that prohibit the ideal relationship. For instance, you might withhold intimacy, be too needy, communicate too much or not enough, or have a fear of commitment. Do any of these sound familiar?

To change this course, you'll need to get rid of the "stuff" you've stored that impacts your heart and mind.

Your unique life experiences.

Recall, there are three things that most impact your life. The world coming in (life) sparks at least one of your five senses, your thoughts are driven by those senses, and the emotions you end up feeling are influenced by those thoughts. So then, how does life need to play out so that you'll feel good more often? The answer to this question has everything to do with your unique experiences.

The experience you have in any given situation is unlike anyone else's. There is not one soul out there that has the same impressions you've had; therefore, they can't possibly have an identical experience. You can also conclude that it is impossible that someone else has the same mindset as you because you've had different experiences and stored them in different ways.

Energy is EVERYTHING.

Why in the world does the mind put those thoughts in your head without your blessing? Because everything in the universe is energy. From the moment the earth was created, it started with a burst of energy. And we, as humans, are made up of constant streams of energy that are created, then stay stagnant or flow freely based on the experiences we've had and how we've allowed our minds to react.

Every experience causes energy inside of you that wants to get out and will find its way out. It's like that raging river flowing fast and furious until it runs into the dam, which changes the patterns and flow. Your experiences of the past and present cause you to store energy. I refer to the energy as "stuff." I've heard others refer to it as "your garbage" that you want to bury and not think about, so you build the dam by storing the stuff that makes you uncomfortable. Storing this stuff takes willpower and even more effort to keep it dormant. It just keeps building up, more and more as you work to store it.

This energy may have originated with a parent who spoke meanly to you or neglected you somehow. Maybe it was a schoolyard bully, a dog that bit you, a time you got lost in the supermarket as a young child, an abusive boss, or a bad breakup when you got "dumped" by the love of your life. Any and all of life's experiences are contributing to your stored energy.

These things happened in your past, and you were not able to effectively deal with the energy. So you stored it, and now it is determining how you will think and feel. What you have now is a subscara, a psychic scar that is often hidden while it blocks the flow of your energy.

The energy eventually makes its way up, and you do one of three things:

1. **You block it.** You get so lost in your thinking mind that you don't really "feel from the heart." The energy is too sensitive, and you'd rather not deal with it. You use your willpower to store the stuff.

2. **You somewhat block it.** You are open to the energy, and you allow it to come up. There are other blockages along the way, but the energy finds its way up as you recall positive things. Imagine the river has become incredibly calm after a giant waterfall. It's just calmly flowing, with no rocks or branches to get in the way. Then, you come across a large rock in the middle of the river that ends the calmness, causing ripples. In this example, those ripples are the emotions you feel, and the rock is your stuff—your stored energy. The rock knows the impressions of your past experiences; it's your subscara that blocks the smooth flow of energy, changing its course. The energy does get through though, as you work to process positive thoughts.

3. **You allow the energy through.** Sometimes, the energy gets past your stuff and runs through you. However, as soon as something happens that hits your subscara, your heart will try to close again.

Sticking with the theme of Relationships from your Mountains for Growth, recall a time when you felt totally in love. You were with someone you adored. Do you remember how you could sit there with that person, just feeling great, a wonderful sensation, a flow of energy, running through your body? That is what it feels like without blockages of stuff. Your heart is open, and life is great.

Let's get back to your mind, that device you are responsible for programming. It wants to help you unblock that energy. That is why it is constantly talking to you, all while you continue to ignore or push the energy down and store it as more stuff.

As an example, assume you walk into a large room full of dozens of people standing around and chatting away. On one side of the room are people you like, and on the other side are people you don't like. What if I asked you to only look at the side of the room that housed the people you like and are most comfortable with and instructed you to never look at the side of the room with those you don't like? Those you are not comfortable with?

What I've just done is separate the room based on what you are comfortable and not comfortable with. At this moment, the side of the room you are not comfortable with doesn't even exist, as it's been buried in your subconscious. It's still there. You are just not aware of it at the moment. But that energy isn't gone. You just buried it with all your other stuff.

However, your mind didn't erase the fact that there are people in the room that you don't like and are not comfortable with. You just buried the energy and will use your willpower to keep it stored away. You do this all the time. When you experience things you don't like, you bury them. Every single day you put more stuff in there, and you use affirmation to confirm that your stuff doesn't exist.

That energy wants out, and it's most likely going to get out through your dreams and your inner voice.

Your dreams release the energy. Sometimes you'll wake and remember them and often wonder why you are dreaming what you are dreaming. The answer lies in the stuff you've stored. The inner voice in your head performs the same function. Consider it your "waking dream," and know that it is working all day long to release energies you've stuffed away. It's your subconscious mind at work, talking, talking, talking all in the spirit of releasing energy, but in doing so, it is interfering with your life.

Don't be so negative.

Have you ever wondered why the voice in your head is so negative? Why, if left unchecked, it will constantly fill your mind with toxic stinkin' thinkin'? The reason is that most of what you've stuffed inside is negative. When you have experiences that remind you of what you've stored (consciously and subconsciously), you then try to stuff even more away, further compounding the negative energy.

You also store experiences you like. However, for most people, what you like pales in comparison to what you don't like. More things tend to turn you off than turn you on. Have you ever tried to pick out paint colors for a room in your house? It is much easier to notice the colors you don't like than those that you do. Why? Because you have an expectation in your mind of what the room should look like. The expectation is based on past experiences, much of which you have buried deep inside of you. And most of the paint colors don't match those expectations. So, you don't like them. In fact, they might even bother you. As I said before, you've set up a system for thinking that makes it difficult to win. It is not your fault. You've created a mindset where more things bother you than turn you on.

You can change this.

Back to your unique life experiences.

Look what you've done! You've created in your mind a rational model of how things should be with respect to all aspects of your life. Consider again your Mountains for Growth. In each area, you have an expectation of where you should be, and when that expectation is not met, what happens? You feel bad. Inside, you are not okay. In some cases, you may feel a sense of struggle or suffering.

Your rational model is made up in your head and is based on your past experiences. Together, they make up a great big lie. That is the lie you tell yourself about how things are supposed to be. You'll actually say, "that was wrong," when things don't go the way you want them to. I am here to tell you that what you made up in your head is NOT how it is supposed to be. The world is an amazing place, and we are blessed to have the gift of life and each breath of air that comes with it. The world around us determines how things are supposed to be. Not you. You have a preference, and that preference drives your thinking, your joy, and your suffering.

A myth exists that the Buddha famously said that all of life is suffering. I'm not a Buddhist, but I know what is meant by this quote, and I imagine you do too. To exist in this world, we must contend with hardship, loss, sadness, and a host of challenges that come with daily living. That's just the way things are. Each of us comes with specific life circumstances and past experiences that lead to our personalized portion of pain. You feel it. I feel it.

So, what's up with the myth? Well, first off, the Buddha didn't speak English. So, any connection to the word suffering was left to interpretation. What the Buddha actually said was, "life is dukkha." The word dukkha has several meanings, and one of those is suffering. However, anything temporary is considered dukkha, including happiness.[3]

The basis of Buddhism is a doctrine known as the Four Noble Truths.[3] The First Truth is that suffering, pain, and misery exist in life. The Second Truth is that this suffering is caused by selfish craving and personal desire (your expectations). The Third Truth is that this selfish craving can be overcome. The Fourth Truth is that the way to overcome this misery is through the Eightfold Path, a series of mindset and behavioral practices.

Why am I sharing this Buddhist lesson? Because it's helpful to understand that not all of life is suffering, but if you don't do the necessary work to manage your expectations, then you will most certainly suffer more than those who do.

The cause of suffering is based on your decision of how you want something to be. The cause of suffering is not the way things are. It's that you decided you wanted it to be a certain way, and it isn't. This suffering comes in various degrees, from relatively mild (barely noticeable) to extreme emotional disturbance that manifests itself for you and others to notice. Both levels come from the same source: your stored energy.

Now consider each of your Mountains for Growth. If your relationship with your mate is not where you thought it would be, or you've not yet found the perfect mate, then you are suffering. If you've not yet achieved the financial freedom you expected at this point in your life, then you'll suffer. If your body doesn't look or feel the way you want it to, you will suffer.

One final word on suffering—recall the happiness equation from earlier; when your results meet your expectations, you will be happier. In other words, when reality doesn't match your expectations, you will suffer. Therefore, managing your expectations is critical to getting and staying on the Success Curve.

Negativity just seems to find me.

The world is full of pessimism that will try to fill your mind with cynicism and negativity. You don't have to go searching for it… simply reading or listening to the news will bring it right to you.

When you succumb to negativity, you risk landing on the Failure Curve, making excuses and blamestorming your way to failure. Unless, of course, you take Brian Tracy's advice and take hold of the one thing you have complete control over—what you think about. Remember, there are two kinds of thoughts: those you create and those your mind creates without you. You are not your mind; you are the witness to the thinking going on in your mind.

Here are three strategies you can use to strengthen your ability to control what you think about and maintain a more positive mindset all while limiting the amount of negativity you let in.

1. **Be intentional with how you start your day.** Avoid beginning your day with negativity. Some of the most successful people I've ever worked with start their day purposely avoiding the news because they know it will infect their minds and get their days off to the wrong start. Obviously, different people have different appetites for their need to stay informed. I recommend limiting morning news consumption as much as possible and being strategic by countering it with something positive. Coming up, I'll share a habit that has made a tremendous difference in my Great Life NOW success and that has helped me to start each day with more positivity, enabling me to be more strategic in how I consume my news. Stay tuned.

2. **Be selective about who you spend your time with and who you give your energy and attention to.** Choose positive people over negative in your friend groups, with your family (when possible), and in who you follow on social media. Once you've identified the

positive and negative influences in your life, you can limit your time with the negative people and spend more time with the positive. Of course, sometimes you can't help but be around toxic thinkers—those who are known for incessantly complaining, gossiping, or putting you or others down—but that doesn't mean you have to actually listen to them. When you find yourself in that situation, consider the source. Toxic, negative thinkers are the same ones who think that being positive is unrealistic. They are the ones who listen to the voice of fear even though the majority of those fears never come to fruition. Think about this: If they are spending most of their time worrying and thinking negatively about stuff that doesn't ever happen, are they really being more realistic in their mode of thinking? Instead of focusing on them, listen to the opinions and advice of people you admire. Not simply like, but admire and respect for their accomplishments, integrity, and work ethic, or because they truly care about you and what you care about.

3. **Be aware of what content you consume.** I mean everything. What music do you listen to? What movies and TV shows do you watch? What books, magazines, blogs, and articles do you read? Does this content inspire you, make you feel confident and smart, or at least leave you in a good mood? Or does it instill fear and worry, and leave you with toxic, negative thoughts?

Let's do a quick consumption check and get you focused on more positivity in your future.

In your workbook . . .

Commit to Consuming Positivity

What are the POSITIVE things you listen to, read, and watch during the day?

What are the NEGATIVE things you listen to, read, and watch during the day?

In what ways can you enhance your approach to consuming information and entertainment?

Replace the voice of fear with the voice of POSITIVITY.

Now that you are paying more attention to what you consume and how it makes you think and feel, let's begin paying attention to what you are saying. Not what you are saying to the outside world, but what you are saying to yourself. The self-talk that we all do each and every day with the inner voice. That voice that, if left unchecked, will generate up to 95% of your thoughts. Do you think that inner voice will have a big impact on your ability to get on and stay on the Success Curve? You bet it will!

It's obvious by now that success begins in your mind, as does failure. It's a powerful device that requires the proper programming for the future. Your past experiences have always impacted the programming. Moving forward, you are going to take control of that device and the programming within it and make the ME Channel one that plays more optimism and less pessimism. This is your choice. You get to decide how you are going to think. What is the mindset you will hold yourself accountable for every day?

Bad stuff is going to happen. Handle it.

Positivity won't prevent negative events from happening. Recall the myth of the Buddha; while all of life is not suffering, life does present us with regular doses of hardship, loss, and sadness. But you control the ME Channel, and you determine how much of the energy you will block or allow to flow freely. When it's flowing freely, you'll achieve more optimism to ensure you respond to those negative events in a positive and productive way.

From my experience, the people who stay on the Success Curve aren't the ones who avoid failure; they're the ones who learn how to respond to failure with optimism. You too can stay on the Success Curve by realizing that negative events are temporary and "they too shall pass." It's also helpful to realize that you can't go back and change anything from your past experiences; all you can do is handle how you react to the event in the present.

Three steps for handling the negative stuff:

1. **Notice it.** When you hear the inner voice being negative, call it out. Literally say, "I hear you." When you cut off the thought, you are stopping it in its tracks.

2. **Take control.** Remember, the one thing you have complete control over in your life is what you think about. So, take control of your response to the negative thought. I recommend taking three calming breaths, then moving on to the third step.

3. **Replace it with an optimistic point of view.** For example, if you are worried about losing your job, then consider that if you did, there are plenty of other opportunities that might lead to even more joy in your life. Or, if you wake up on the weekend and see that it is cloudy and rainy, then consider that you finally have the time to watch that movie you have been putting off seeing. A simple reframe will enable more positive energy and emotion.

You get the point... find the positive. If you try, you'll almost always find something. You are not being unrealistic. You are being realistically positive by focusing on channeling your energy towards a positive mindset that will enhance your mood and keep you on the Success Curve.

Practice won't make you perfect, but it will make you better.

With so much negativity around us each day, you can expect that if you quit your daily discipline of consuming positivity and practicing optimism, you will soon revert to the stinkin' thinkin' of negative thoughts. It doesn't seem fair, does it?

> **Your psyche is like any other muscle, and it needs to be exercised, or it loses its strength.**

If you've been working out and getting your body in shape, you can't stop working out and expect to keep the same physique. Within a short period of time, your muscles will lose their tone and shape. If you've been running five miles three times a week and you stop, guess what? The next time you head out for a run, you will be sucking wind by the end of the first mile.

It is the same for your mind. When reading, writing, thinking, and problem-solving are part of your daily life, your mind is sharp. You are controlling more of the inner voice. It is in shape, just like your body is after regular exercise. However, if you were to take an extended break from doing the things that keep your mind sharp, over time, it will get a little soft, and it may take you a few days to get it back in shape.

My point is this: It takes consistent practice to become better at controlling your mind and emotions. If it didn't, we'd all be positive thinkers. So, don't resist the need to practice being positive, especially when it takes so little effort to try to consume positivity and control your thoughts each day.

Make the shift from scarcity to abundance thinking.

Every step of your Great Life NOW journey thus far has positioned you to make a shift in mindset from scarcity to abundance. These two modes of thinking are vastly different, and your success living a Great Life NOW depends, in part, on which mindset you adopt.

A mindset of scarcity is when you focus, usually unconsciously, on what is lacking or wrong in your life. For example, those living on Someday Island tend to think, "I'll be happy when," which keeps them in a constant mode of scarcity. A scarcity mindset puts you in a place of continual worry, anxiety, fear, and insecurity, and you tend to blame other people or your circumstances for your reality. An abundance mindset allows you to do just the opposite by focusing on what is, why it is good, and the positive outcomes that may be achieved.

Just like all your other thinking patterns, scarcity and abundance are driven by your past experiences. They are part of your thinking system, driven by fear and expectations for the future. If you are to excel in your Mountains for Growth, you'll need to choose an abundance mindset and stay away from scarcity thinking.

Scarcity comes in two forms. One is flight, in which we seek to protect ourselves from an unsafe world by retreating into a comfort zone to avoid failure and rejection. When you are in "flight," you play it safe and avoid competing for fear of losing. The second form of scarcity is to fight for more success. "Fight" is seeking to "win" at life by achieving more and accumulating more, whether in the form of power, status, money, or things. When you're in the "fight" form of scarcity, you're trying to win at life and don't realize that, in most cases, you're only competing against yourself.

In both forms, life becomes like a roller coaster where you feel good when things go well and bad when things do not go your way. Regardless of how you are feeling, there just seems to be never-ending uneasiness, frustration, worry, doubt, and inadequacy about what is wrong or could go wrong. Your life feels more difficult than it needs to be. You are suffering on Someday Island and don't know why.

If you stay in the scarcity mode of thinking, it is very difficult to get off the Failure Curve and onto the Success Curve.

On the other hand, those who primarily operate with the mindset of abundance more often predict and create their own reality on the Success Curve to goal achievement.

Choosing the abundance mode of thinking means focusing on what is right in your life. You see the positivity in most situations, focusing on what is or what could be rather than what is not, what is missing, or what is lacking.

In abundance mode, you are not being unrealistic, you are being realistically positive. When in this mode, you will still experience negative emotions, thoughts, and situations; however, you will simply choose not to remain in a negative mindset or situation. Abundance thinkers maintain faith that things happen for a reason and that good will come about.

Abundance thinkers realize that they need to crush their fears, leverage their Strengths, and work daily to bring their values to life. Doing so helps them move their mountains. Be an abundance thinker. It makes life so much better. It makes life Great.

From my experience, the big difference between the scarcity and abundance thinker is how they manage their beliefs.

Abundance thinkers focus on what is "right" in life.

Activate Empowering Beliefs.

Our beliefs are strong feelings of certainty. They are ideas we hold to be true, regardless of empirical evidence. Those with an abundance mindset believe they have the resources and resourcefulness needed to be successful. They know "if it's to be, it's up to me," and they take ownership of their success rather than make excuses for their failures.

If you want to live a Great Life NOW—one where you are performing at your best, maximizing your happiness, managing your fears, leveraging your Strengths, and living your values—then you must take control of your life-shaping mindset and activate beliefs that empower you. You'll do this by developing and sustaining a "choose the positive" attitude, which is more than a quick-fix motivational technique. Instead, it's a disciplined skill you will practice every day for the rest of your life.

You don't become what you want, you become what you believe.

-Oprah Winfrey

Abundance thinkers focus on what is "right" in life.

Activate Empowering Beliefs.

Our beliefs are strong feelings of certainty. They are ideas we hold to be true, regardless of empirical evidence. Those with an abundance mindset believe they have the resources and resourcefulness needed to be successful. They know "if it's to be, it's up to me," and they take ownership of their success rather than make excuses for their failures.

If you want to live a Great Life NOW—one where you are performing at your best, maximizing your happiness, managing your fears, leveraging your Strengths, and living your values—then you must take control of your life-shaping mindset and activate beliefs that empower you. You'll do this by developing and sustaining a "choose the positive" attitude, which is more than a quick-fix motivational technique. Instead, it's a disciplined skill you will practice every day for the rest of your life.

You don't become what you want, you become what you believe.

-Oprah Winfrey

In both forms, life becomes like a roller coaster where you feel good when things go well and bad when things do not go your way. Regardless of how you are feeling, there just seems to be never-ending uneasiness, frustration, worry, doubt, and inadequacy about what is wrong or could go wrong. Your life feels more difficult than it needs to be. You are suffering on Someday Island and don't know why.

If you stay in the scarcity mode of thinking, it is very difficult to get off the Failure Curve and onto the Success Curve.

On the other hand, those who primarily operate with the mindset of abundance more often predict and create their own reality on the Success Curve to goal achievement.

Choosing the abundance mode of thinking means focusing on what is right in your life. You see the positivity in most situations, focusing on what is or what could be rather than what is not, what is missing, or what is lacking.

In abundance mode, you are not being unrealistic, you are being realistically positive. When in this mode, you will still experience negative emotions, thoughts, and situations; however, you will simply choose not to remain in a negative mindset or situation. Abundance thinkers maintain faith that things happen for a reason and that good will come about.

Abundance thinkers realize that they need to crush their fears, leverage their Strengths, and work daily to bring their values to life. Doing so helps them move their mountains. Be an abundance thinker. It makes life so much better. It makes life Great.

From my experience, the big difference between the scarcity and abundance thinker is how they manage their beliefs.

STEP 2 : Find your Empowering Beliefs.

Replace each Limiting Belief with an Empowering Belief

EXAMPLE:

Limiting Belief: I don't have enough education to get that job.

Empowering Belief: The truth is that my work experience exceeds my education, and I am more than qualified.

1.

Limiting Belief:

Empowering Belief:

2.

Limiting Belief:

Empowering Belief:

3.

Limiting Belief:

Empowering Belief:

In your workbook . . .

Activate Empowering Beliefs

Now that you've chosen a positivity mindset and abundance thinking, it's time to pave your way forward by addressing Limiting Beliefs that hold you back while also creating Empowering Beliefs to catapult you forward.

Beliefs, like the fears you addressed earlier, are based on past experiences that have molded your thinking. Beliefs are critical to getting on and staying on the Success Curve as they are a primary ingredient that will influence your behaviors, goals, and habits.

STEP 1 : Recognize Limiting Beliefs.

A Limiting Belief is something you believe to be true that restricts you in some way. The belief could be about you, other people, or your circumstances in life or the world. These beliefs may hold you back from making important choices, keep you from seeing opportunities, or prevent you from leveraging your Strengths and capabilities. If not addressed, your Limiting Beliefs will push you down the Failure Curve, filling your life with a scarcity mindset packed with worry, anxiety, indecision, and consistently negative thoughts.

What are **three Limiting Beliefs** that have been producing unwanted or negative consequences in your life?

Limiting Belief:	Negative consequences I experience as a result of the Limiting Belief:
1.	
2.	
3.	

Activating GOALS & HABITS

The only way to change is to first make the decision to change.

A Great Life NOW doesn't just happen—it comes from thinking, planning, and pursuing what is most important to you. You've created your Purpose, discovered your Strengths and Superpowers, explored and positioned yourself to crush your fears, and committed to living The Brand Called YOU with a focus on your Mountains for Growth. And you've chosen to move forward with more control over what you think about with a renewed mindset of positivity and Empowering Beliefs that will help you knock down barriers and run with opportunities.

NOW is the time to put your Great Life NOW Game Plan into action by clarifying what you want, the desired results you'll feel great about, and the necessary thoughts and actions to make your vision of success a reality.

Clarity on What, Why, and How.

As Zig Ziglar famously said, "If you aim at nothing, you'll hit it every time." So, think of goals as serving the purpose of providing you WHAT you are aiming for. That's it, nothing more, nothing less. Let's not overcomplicate things.

Scientific research shows that setting and working toward goals can contribute to happiness in a variety of ways that include creating motivation, engagement, and pleasure, and instilling a sense of accomplishment and confidence in what we can do in the future.[4]

What I've found is that while goals serve the purpose of briefly focusing our attention and setting direction, the real source of happiness comes from the journey to accomplish those goals.

For decades, consultants and personal development gurus have advocated for numerous goal development models. I've followed and tested out a few of them in my past and found them to be helpful in organizing my thinking and plans. One of the most logical and widely used models is the S.M.A.R.T. goals framework, which states that goals should have five qualities: Specific (clearly state what it is you want to achieve), Measurable (determine ways to measure whether you are making progress), Attainable (make sure it is realistic and achievable), Relevant (ensure it is meaningful to your life), Time-bound (commit to when you will achieve it).

I applaud this framework for its simplicity and for helping people to do the initial thinking required to set the direction for achieving what's most important to them.

However, documentation of the goal is the easy part and only gets you a small way forward. The real benefit to you in achieving a Great Life NOW is knowing HOW to accomplish your goals in ways that allow for success in each of the focus areas for growth. The HOW is in the habits!

I am not downplaying the importance of having goals. They are a must along your journey. Without them, you wouldn't know WHAT you want to achieve. But I am suggesting that the road to achieving your goals is considerably more important, and that road consists of the habits you will commit to. As a matter of fact, you will see that once you set your goal, if you completely ignore it moving forward and only focus on the habits, you will most likely still succeed. Your habits fuel the progress that drives happiness.

So, when it comes to your goals, I say, “Set it and forget it” and focus on the habits instead. We’re going to keep your goals really simple. You are not going to overthink them. You simply need to state WHAT you want to achieve with respect to your Mountains for Growth.

Do you want to run a marathon or lose 20 pounds? Do you want to create more mindfulness by reflecting for 15 minutes each day? Improve a relationship? Be more productive at work? Achieve a promotion? Save a million dollars? Buy a lake house? Volunteer for a charity?

There are a variety of goals you could create for each of your Mountains for Growth focus areas. You just need to determine what you want and ensure it is truly meaningful and that achieving it will create happiness. You’ll do this by aligning your goals with your Purpose, Superpowers, Brand, and Beliefs.

Once you have articulated your goal, you will dive into the mindset and actions required to ensure you make significant progress in achieving it.

Coming up, you’ll learn a five-part framework to make any goal come to life. And the reason you will be successful is because you will design it for success.

Consider this: Every Olympic athlete wants to win a gold medal. Every candidate wants to get the job. Every salesperson wants to make their quota. And if successful and unsuccessful people share the same type of goals, then the goal cannot be what differentiates the winners from the losers. I would argue that it is the positive, daily habits that separate the winners from the losers in the game of life.

Those who know HOW to achieve their goals and practice the daily and weekly habits are the ones who continuously improve and achieve the best outcomes.

It's the positive, daily habits that separate the winners from the losers in the game of life.

Your success has EVERYTHING to do with your thinking and doing habits.

Your habits determine how GREAT your life will be. Your habits are nothing more than thoughts or actions that you repeat over and over until they become automatic and almost effortless. We humans are creatures of habit, and each day we are directed by hundreds of them. It's simply part of being human. Would it surprise you to know that 95% of our thoughts and 45% of our behaviors are habitual?[5] That's right: Most of what we think about and almost half of our daily actions are done because that's the way we've always done them!

You will either create positive rituals, routines, and behaviors (habits) that help you live The Brand Called YOU and reach your goals, or you'll develop negative habits that bring challenges and lost opportunities.

Creating a habit can be both simple and easy to do. Unfortunately, in many cases, it's just as easy to not do it, which is why the Activation process is needed.

There are two types of habits that will ensure you are living a Great Life NOW. And make no mistake, the quality of your life depends on the quality of these habits:

- **Thinking habits:** Your thoughts.
- **Doing habits:** Your actions.

Therefore, to live a Great Life NOW, you have to be much more intentional about your thinking and doing habits. Remember, your mind is an incredible gift that thinks about what you tell it to think about. The choice is yours.

Some habits you design into your Great Life NOW Game Plan may take you out of your comfort zone. That is okay. In fact, getting out of your comfort zone is a good thing. You'll see that comfort doesn't lead to happiness. Growth through your habits and progress leads to more happiness.

The secret formula for happiness:

HABITS + PROGRESS =

HAPPINESS

So, let's get intentional in how you will think and do so you can move your mountains forward!

Most people fail when attempting to change their habits. You won't! Those who fail don't have the right thinking system, or they don't understand "who they are" and why their Core Values are so important. You've done the work. You've made your rules. You are ready for habit-building success! It's within you. That's the difference between your efforts now and those failed efforts of the past. Now, you've defined who you are so the new habits can become part of this identity. In the past, you'd say, "I want to create this habit." Now, you are ready to say, "I am this habit. It is part of who I am."

The more pride you have in The Brand Called YOU, the more motivated you will be to master your habits. Once you become proud, you'll commit to the staying power necessary to demonstrate your habits. Think about other areas of your life you take pride in. Do you take pride in the paintings you create? Then you are more likely to spend hours painting each week. Do you take pride in having that six-pack of abs? Then you most likely work out a few days a week. Do you take pride in your job status? Then you make sure you put in the few extra hours at the beginning or end of the day.

Sustainable habit change requires that you close the "identity gap" that exists between who you are today and who you will become. You will find that as this gap closes, your habits will embody The Brand Called YOU. When you demonstrate each one, you are playing by your rules, bringing those values to life. The more you repeat the thinking (mindset) and behaviors behind your habits, the more you reinforce The Brand Called YOU. As the evidence accumulates, you'll continue to make progress up the Success Curve, and the identity gap will close.

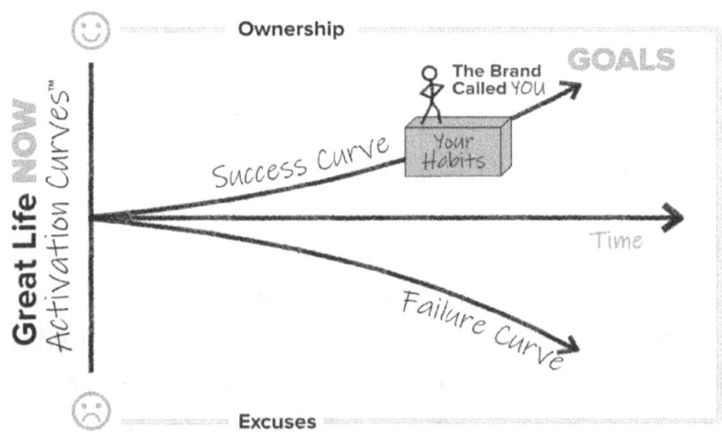

Over time, you'll begin to think of your daily habits as the fuel of success, and you'll start to see more clearly how they keep you on the Success Curve and pave the way to ensure you are making progress moving your mountains.

A little more time will pass, your habits will continue to reinforce your beliefs about yourself, and before you know it... BAM!!!... you'll actually become The Brand Called YOU.

The habit-building process below is a proven, step-by-step approach to designing strategic, high-impact habits that will bring The Brand Called YOU to life while helping you create more self-worth and move those mountains forward.

Are you ready to activate your first goal?

In this next section, you will activate your first goal and set of habits. Toward the end, you will have the opportunity to activate a few more.

There are five steps to activating and sustaining habits to reach your goals. Trust me when I tell you that you don't want to skip any of the five steps. If you do, I can assure you there will be predictable consequences, i.e., you will struggle to make the habit stick, making goal achievement much more difficult, if not impossible. So, why take the chance? Plan to complete each step. You will find that all of the key elements of the S.M.A.R.T. goal-setting method are covered, plus you'll have the required thinking and doing habits to virtually guarantee success. (More on this idea of a "guarantee" in a few minutes.) Keep reading to learn the process, and then we'll put it into action.

The only way to change is to first make the decision to change.

In your workbook . . .

Your What, Why, and How

In this exercise you will be guided through a **five-step Habit Activation Process.**

STEP 1 : Describe what you want (the goal you want to achieve).

In this step, describe the results or actions you want to see happen in your life and when you want to see them happen. You'll want to be specific and ensure the results or actions are achievable. Don't make the goal too much of a stretch. Aspirational goals are fine, just make sure there is more realism than aspiration. Like most things in life, it's a balancing act.

Use these questions to help you set your goal:

- Which of your Mountains for Growth will be most impacted?
- What mindset and/or empowering beliefs will be most helpful?
- What strengths are you uniquely suited to leverage (or further develop)?
- What belief(s) will most empower you?

Remember, be specific. You'll want to be sure to include a reasonable amount of description. You wouldn't sit down in a hairdresser's chair and say, "Cut my hair." You'd want to be specific about what you want it to look like. If you were shopping for a new home, you wouldn't tell the realtor, "Find me a house." You'd want to describe the type of home you're most interested in.

So, don't write down a goal that you want to "be healthier." Instead, write down what you want to achieve that you think will lead you to a healthier lifestyle; for example, "Work out five days a week." Or, don't simply write that you want to "be happier" or "be more productive" or "achieve financial freedom" (can you tell I've seen these before?). Instead, be specific and write down what you want to achieve that you believe will lead you to more happiness, or make you more productive, or cause you to feel as though you've reached your financial aspirations.

Lastly, make a commitment to what you feel is a reasonable amount of time to achieve your goal. Have a deadline and consider including some key milestones along the way. As you check off those milestones, you'll be recognizing the progress that powers your happiness. Remember, it's the journey, not the destination.

What do you want? Document your goal.

STEP 2: Know your WHY (the benefit to your life).

How is achieving your goal going to positively influence your life? Quite often, you'll find the content of your goal may be less important to your overall well-being than your reasons for pursuing it. Here is your chance to clearly state why achieving this goal is important to you.

In order to discover why the goal matters, consider the following questions:

- What specific benefits will you experience in your personal life? In your work life?
- If you don't achieve the goal, what consequences might you face?

- How will achieving the goal make a positive difference in your life?
- How will achieving the goal make a positive difference in the lives of others?

Why is this goal a benefit to you?

STEP 3 : Design the habits (the thoughts and actions required) to fuel your success.

Remember, a Great Life NOW does not happen by chance, it happens by design. You are in the design phase where success is completely up to you. You get to determine your habits for how you will think and what you will do.

You will find that you have complete control of these habits—that is, at first. Then they will become automatic and take on a life of their own. This is a very good thing as they will become second nature, happening with little effort, yet powerfully propelling you up the Success Curve.

What thoughts, rituals, routines, or behaviors should you commit to because they will cause your success over time?

List all repeated actions that will support you on your journey to achieving what you want (your goal).

Document the HOW. What are your thinking and doing habits?

Before moving on to Step 4: Generating Staying Power, there are two secrets for you to know that will help ensure your success.

Two secrets for your success in designing and performing your habits.

Secret #1: The Power of One Percent.

In the introduction of the Great Life NOW journey, I shared that if you want to see improvement in your life—whether that's in your relationships, career, health, or finances—then you have to get better. For things to change, you have to change. For things to improve, you have to improve.

I introduced the concept of the Power of One Percent and kept it very simple. We imagined that if you got one percent better every day at anything you wanted to accomplish, you would end up 365 percent better by the end of the year. Simple addition, without consideration for compounding interest.

I shared this simple perspective to whet your appetite, knowing that when we got to the exciting step of designing the habits that will positively change your life, the realities of the Power of One Percent could surprise you.

If you were to truly get 1% better each day in any of your areas of focus, you'd become more than 37 times better in a year. That's right, with a little effort in making small, if not tiny, improvements on a daily basis, you can improve the outcome from any habit by an astounding amount.

People often underestimate the power of well-designed habits and falsely believe they need to take on massive action with huge time commitments. However, in most cases, your goal can be reached (whether it's losing weight, learning a new skill, running a half marathon, or any other goal) by committing to small, actionable, daily habits that help you make progress toward large, yet attainable, goals.

It is easy to dismiss the power of progress when making small, incremental improvements daily. Don't fall victim to missing the progress along the way. Remember, progress is an essential ingredient in the formula for happiness.

How to get 37 times better in one year.

Let's assume you begin the year with $100, and with a little bit of effort toward your daily habits, you can increase the value of that money by 1% each day. At the end of the year, you'd have $3,778.34. That's an increase of 37 times. Now that is the power of compounding! ($100* (1+1%) ^365)

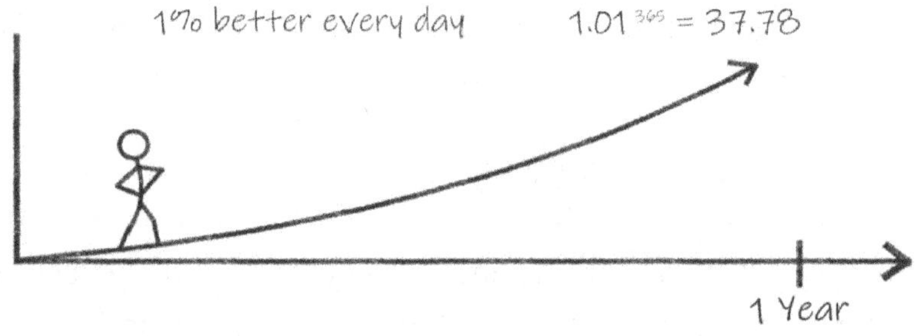

Your small efforts don't seem to make much of a difference on a daily basis, but added up over the weeks, months, and years, your daily disciplined habits compound into significant success in the long-term. The graph looks a lot like your desired Success Curve, doesn't it?

Now, suppose you wanted to become an expert in investing or real estate... or pick any subject that will help you on your Great Life NOW journey. What if you agreed to the habit of reading 10 pages on the subject each day, every single day, for one year? Wouldn't that lead you down the pathway of significant knowledge, positioning you to sprint up the Success Curve? Those 10 pages a day would compound to 3,650 pages or the equivalent of a few dozen books of career or life-changing know-how. Would you grow and improve in that subject? Would you have more opportunities for success moving forward in one of your Mountains for Growth? You absolutely would!

That's the idea with the Power of One Percent. Once you have a goal in place, determine what habits you want to deploy your energy and focus on and commit to at least a small amount of effort each day.

Keep in mind, successful people do what unsuccessful people are not willing to do. And they do it with small amounts of effort, as little as 1% each day.

Successful people do what unsuccessful people are not willing to do. And they do it with small amounts of effort, as little as 1% each day.

The next secret to your habit-sustaining success is to learn to block your time.

Secret #2: Time block to make the time.

Regardless of your goal or the habits to support it, it can be easy to fall victim to the Raging River of Responsibility and use lack of time as an excuse.

It can be easy to put off doing just about any of your

commitments, even if you know it is the most important thing you can do today to reach your goals for tomorrow.

The secret to staying on track, moving up the Success Curve, is to block your time. Time blocking is the simple task of scheduling an appointment with you and your habit. It's easy, and you can apply it to every goal in your Great Life NOW Game Plan.

Simply go to your calendar and "block the time" you need to perform your habit each day or week. Color code it if you can so that it stands out as different from the typical appointments you have during the day. If appropriate for your specific habit, make this time as early as you can in your day, when your mind is fresh, and when you are less likely to have something else come up that will steal that time from you. If you are unable to block big chunks of time, then start small. Remember the Power of One Percent is working for you. Also, remember that you are charting a course up the Success Curve, and doing so requires small, daily, disciplined habits that you can make progress on over time—progress that makes you happy.

Make a commitment to yourself that there are no cancellations allowed. If, for some reason, you need to skip the appointment you've scheduled for your habit, then make sure to reschedule it.

Next, schedule a 30-minute block of time each week to review your progress. Ask yourself:

1. Based on my success last week, what could I do this week to improve even more?
2. Do I have enough time blocked off next week?
3. Based on my success to date, do I need to alter my expectations for my habits or goals?

After a few weeks of time blocking, you'll become even better at forecasting the time needed to perform your habits and achieve your goals. And you'll be witnessing your progress along the way.

STEP 4 : Demonstrate staying power (the willpower to overcome the obstacles).

Sustaining your new habits will require a little extra thought and energy to get going. And part of this extra energy and thought requires you to plan for the inevitable willpower obstacles. Before I get into what I mean by willpower obstacles, I want to warn you: this is the step that most people are tempted to skip. DON'T! Skipping this step leads to predictable consequences. Ignoring the willpower obstacles will make it very difficult to keep the consistency going with your chosen rituals, routines, and behaviors that make up your habit.

Willpower is the ability to do what really matters, even when at times it might seem difficult. Running out of willpower can ruin your habit.

Willpower is interesting. As it turns out, our willpower is in short supply each day and deteriorates when we get stressed and tired. So, with the design of any habit, you must predict where and when you might run out of willpower. Where might you be tempted to forget or simply decide not to do it? Predicting where you may fail is not an act of being negative. You are actually taking initiative to be self-compassionate, which will increase your chances of success over time.

Researchers and scientists who make a living studying human behavior tell us that around 77% of people maintain focus on a goal for a week or less and then slip back into old routines and habits.[6]

All too often, when we don't see a positive change right away, we struggle to keep the commitments we make to ourselves. In this case, you may end up with a few too many excuses for why you can't keep your Great Life NOW commitments.

Let's not let that happen!

Predict where you might run out. When might you be tempted to forget or say, "Aw, screw it"? Review your rituals, routines, and behaviors from Step 3 to ensure you have the right ones to overcome the eventual willpower obstacles and add new ones as necessary.

Life is filled with joy, happiness, and good fortune when you develop "staying power." For most, getting started is the easy part. Let's call it your "starting power." You, like most, may find it is plentiful when it comes to kickstarting a new habit, but it's those who think about and address the willpower obstacles that increase their staying power, especially when adversity strikes (and it will). Your staying power is what you want more of as it will keep you on the Success Curve or at least help you get back on it when you fall off.

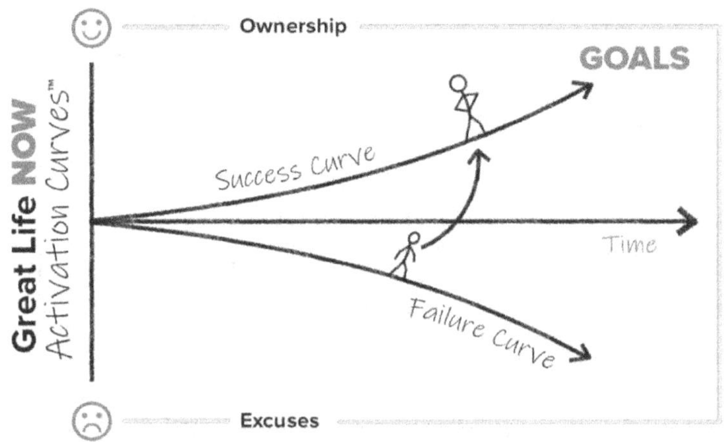

What obstacles might threaten your staying power?

STEP 5: Ask every day, "Did I try?"

Now we've arrived at the fifth and final step. Congratulations on getting this far. You are almost there! You can't stop now though. The fifth and final step will guarantee your success. That's right, I just said GUARANTEE. We all know there are very few guarantees in life. Ben Franklin famously gave us two things he said were certain in life: death and taxes. Well, I am about to give you a third certainty, a true guarantee that you will make progress on performing your habits. But to get the guarantee, you need to do a tiny bit of work.

For each of the habits you've documented, take a few seconds each day to ask yourself, "Did I TRY?"

Take notice: You are not asking yourself whether you actually performed the habit. You're asking whether you even tried. If you do this for five seconds a day, I GUARANTEE you will improve! I can guarantee that you will make positive progress and get better at whatever thinking or doing habit you've designed in any of your areas of focus, which will lead to at least some of the benefits you've been thinking about.

That's it, only a few seconds each day to rewire your brain, reinforcing your desired habit is a high priority. The reality is, what we track determines where we focus and what we are motivated to improve. Daily tracking, for even a few seconds a day, will ensure you take the time to reflect on your "HOW" rituals, routines, and behaviors. And I guarantee, over time, you will make progress, and you will get better. You will become even happier.

This idea of daily tracking is not a new concept. In fact, it was Ben Franklin, more than 250 years ago, who mastered daily tracking to accomplish tremendous success in life. One could easily make the case that Ben Franklin is one of the most accomplished humans ever! Here are a few of his accomplishments:

- One of the founding fathers of America
- Mapped the Gulf Stream
- Created bifocal glasses and the Franklin stove
- Invented the flexible catheter
- Spearheaded and greatly influenced many staples we take for granted today, including the first library for lending books, the first public hospital, and the first university back in 1749[7]

These are a few of his many accomplishments in a lifetime packed with tremendous, innovative successes. How did he do all of this?

Late in his life, Franklin wrote his autobiography and attributed his ability to set and track daily thoughts and behaviors as his secret to success. That's right; he attributed his lifetime of successes to his daily effort to track as a method for self-improvement.

Here is what Ben Franklin did: He created 13 virtues to guide how he would think and act. Each of his virtues led him towards a series of thoughts and behaviors he felt were important. His virtues included things like: be sincere, demonstrate justice, have high resolve, demonstrate moderation, and be humble. These virtues were his version of The Brand Called YOU.

According to his autobiography, he focused on one virtue each week. And each day of the week, he tracked the virtue as to whether he "lived it," asking himself, "Did I do it?" At the end of the week, he would review how many days he felt he had demonstrated the virtue. Then he would pick another virtue for the next week. He would cycle through each virtue four times during the year.

Now Ben Franklin, for all his successes that have benefited our world, was not perfect. Far from it. In fact, while one of his virtues was chastity, he was known to be quite the philanderer. He wrote about his extramarital affairs in his memoir. Like all of us, he was a work in progress. Ben Franklin understood the key ingredient to successfully mastering habits: progress, not perfection! He lived his brand most of the time. But he was far from perfect.

Maybe Ben Franklin from the mid-to late 1700s is simply too far back. Want another example?

Can becoming funny be a habit? Jerry Seinfeld thinks so. In my opinion, Seinfeld could be regarded as one of the funniest humans ever. When asked by a reporter how he became so funny, he shared his daily tracking approach to creating the habit of thinking about and writing humorous material. His approach is called "Don't Break the Chain."

I'm paraphrasing what Seinfeld said in response to being asked how he became so funny. He said that before he became famous for his TV show, he was just trying to survive by doing standup comedy at local clubs. He had a strong desire to become funnier. So, he began to force himself to write down something funny every day. He purchased a large desk calendar and each month would tape it up on his bedroom wall. Then, each day, he would try to write down one thing he saw or thought of that he thought was funny. Over time, he made thinking about and writing down funny ideas a habit. And collected a ton of material in the process.

Seinfeld practiced the Power of One Percent and became exponentially better at his craft. Did he get 37 times funnier every year he practiced this habit? Maybe. Maybe not. But he sure did achieve historic levels of acclaim as a comedian and actor who co-created and starred in what *TV Guide* ranked as the "second greatest TV show of all time."[8]

So, what do these examples mean to you? Well, for one, you are not trying to become one of the most accomplished humans ever or the funniest person in the world. You are simply trying to master a habit that aligns with your brand, and helps you move your mountains forward. And daily tracking by taking a few seconds to consider your effort ("Did I try?") will guarantee you improve and stay on the Success Curve to a Great Life NOW.

And tracking has never been easier.

There is an app for that.

In fact, tons of apps exist for daily habit tracking. Simply visit the app store on your smartphone and search the topic of "habit tracking." You will find a variety of apps, and many of them are free.

Download a habit-tracking app that enables you to set a daily reminder that will encourage you to stop and take a few seconds to think about your commitment to your Great Life NOW journey.

What matters most is
CONSISTENCY OVER TIME
not the intensity of consecutive days
or weeks performing your new habits.

It doesn't matter whether you are trying to eat a healthy snack after lunch, read a real estate article each morning, or become a better listener. To make something habitual, you need to take a daily inventory of your thoughts, words, and actions.

Time to activate more goals and habits.

You've come so far! You've learned the five-step activation process for goals and habits. As mentioned before, you will not be one of those people who fails at attempting to reach ill-thought-out goals because you know how to describe WHAT you want, document WHY you want it, and list the habits (the HOW) for achievement. Following each of the five steps will guarantee you make progress up the Success Curve, ensuring you are living a Great Life NOW.

The Power of PROGRESS (NOT Perfection)

Next, go to your Great Life NOW workbook and clarify your top three to five goals and accompanying habits to activate in the coming months and years.

> **Nothing will work unless you do.**
>
> -Maya Angelou

In your workbook . . .

Your What, Why, and How (Goals, Benefits, and Habits)

GOAL (what you want; be specific)	HABITS (routines and behaviors)
Why (benefit to you)	

Watch out for a few pitfalls.

You are ready to sprint forward, create even more self-worth, and move your mountains forward. However, before you jump into activating your new goals and habits, let's cover some of the pitfalls to watch out for. From years of observation, coupled with reviewing dozens of research studies on why people find it hard to stick to good habits, I've organized four common pitfalls.

1. "It's just not enjoyable."

The decision to start a new habit and make a change often feels good even before anything has changed. You've done nothing yet, but you get a warm, nice feeling. However, people often give up quickly and without as much guilt when the habit they are trying to form simply does not provide joy. Remember to take the time to reflect on your WHY of achieving the goal. Remember how it will positively impact your life and the consequences you can avoid by changing your actions.

2. We are obsessed with instant gratification.

In general, we want things now rather than later. There is a psychological discomfort associated with self-denial. As humans, we are wired with a desire for instant gratification. Remember… quite often we want it immediately, if not sooner. We have the natural-born instinct to seize the rewards at hand. This is even further fueled by technology that enables us to binge-watch our favorite shows ("No way am I waiting a week to see what happens next") and order almost anything online for same-day delivery—or at least two days to your door. Want to go on a date? Swipe right!

The possibilities for fulfilling our instant gratification are endless. However, no genuine success in life is instant. Life is not a clickable link. In almost everything we do, we expect overnight transformation and success after one day (or a few days). When it comes to seeing and feeling the benefits of your chosen habits, it often takes time, often weeks, months, or even years. A Great Life NOW is not a program. It's not a temporary change you are making. It's a never-ending journey to a new way of thinking, speaking, and acting… a new way of being. Many of the habits on your journey will require you to demonstrate patience.

3. Our goals are too lofty.

When planning to take on a habit that will be meaningful personally and/or professionally, we tend to get excited and put goals and habits in place that are simply too difficult to achieve. You'll want to ensure your commitments are both meaningful and attainable. If you make them too much of a stretch, the excuse machine is much easier to start up.

4. "Aw, screw this, it's not worth the effort."

The difference between the people who make habits stick and those who don't often comes down to their attitude toward slip-ups. People who fail have an all-or-nothing mentality. It's not whether you slip up, it's how you handle it that matters. The "Aw, screw it" pitfall is a close cousin to the instant gratification one noted previously. There is a scientific take on this phenomenon, called the What-the-Hell Effect, which explains why people are so likely to give up a new habit because of a slip-up. The What-the-Hell Effect describes the cycle you feel when you indulge, regret what you've done, and then go back for more.[9] The phrase was coined by dieting researchers, but the effect can apply to any setback or willpower challenge. What happens is your brain rationalizes your behavior. For instance, suppose you are dieting and come across a plate of cookies, and you eat one. Next, you tell yourself, "You already blew your goal of not eating sweets, so, what the hell, you might as well eat the entire plate." According to Kelly McGonigal, who writes about the effect in *The Willpower Instinct*, "Giving in makes you feel bad about yourself, which motivates you to do something to feel better. And what's the cheapest, fastest strategy for feeling better? Often the very thing you feel bad about… It's not the first giving-in that guarantees the bigger relapse. It's the feelings of shame, guilt, loss of control, and loss of hope that follow the first relapse."[10]

Watch out for the "Aw, screw it" pitfall and What-the-Hell Effect when it comes to your habits. If you miss a day, a week, or even a few weeks, don't worry about it. The most important thing is to acknowledge how you respond when you realize that you've let yourself down. Do you automatically shift into self-criticism and beat yourself up over losing control? Most people do, which only fuels the feelings of guilt or the excuses you tell yourself as to why you've not performed your habit. The trick is to shift into a mindset of self-compassion and realize instead that what matters is consistency over time.

Expect to course-correct.

How about another guarantee? Here you go… my second guarantee for you. You will absolutely need to course-correct over time and do so often.

Consider a flight from New York to San Diego. That's about six hours, and you'll keep busy reading, sleeping, or watching a movie, but at no time will you question whether the flight will land in San Diego. You don't get on that flight thinking it will end up in Texas, Arizona, Idaho, or anywhere else that isn't on your itinerary. In fact, if the pilot were to announce you were heading in the wrong direction, you'd be more than a little freaked out. But here's the surprising part: Even though the pilot doesn't make those announcements, the plane is heading in the wrong direction over 90% of the flight.[11]

You know how the in-flight channel with the map shows your progress and makes it look like you're flying in a straight line? The truth is... you are not. The plane zigzags regularly, making constant course corrections. The pilot never mentions it, because it happens hundreds of times along the way and is totally normal. These adjustments happen to account for air pressure, weather, the changing weight of the plane as fuel is consumed, or simply new information about flight traffic. All of these course corrections are part of a normal flight from point A to point B.

Why am I sharing this with you? How does it impact your Great Life NOW journey?

Just as with flying a plane to the destination you want to reach, the key to performing your habits consistently and reaching your goals is to have checkpoints along the way to determine your progress and to have a willingness to course-correct when things change. Make sure to do each step in the Goals and Habits Activation process, including the daily tracking of your effort level ("Did I try?"), and be willing to forgive yourself when adversity strikes. The important thing is to course-correct and get back on track, and before you know it, you will land at your destination having mastered the habit, and ultimately, you will reach your goals.

In your workbook . . .

Adversity Will Strike—What to Do About It

Any adult who has lived a couple of hours in the real world knows that at least a little adversity strikes along the journey to any stated goals. There may even be times when you feel you are sliding down the Failure Curve.

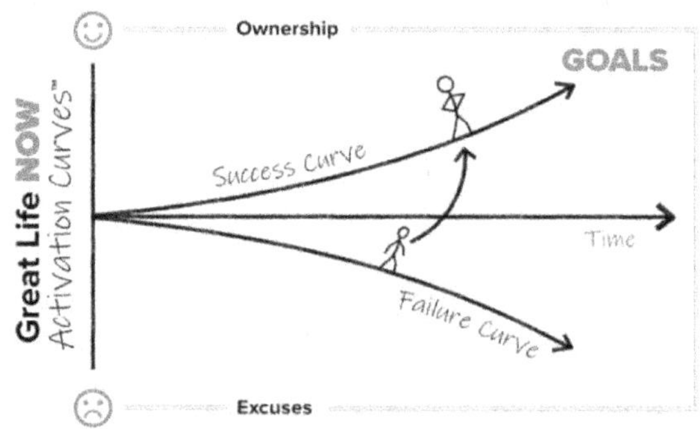

The key to your success will not be avoiding failure, but rather, knowing what to do when you get knocked down by an obstacle. What will you do to get back on the Success Curve?

Take a moment to consider the obstacles that might knock you down and list the specific mindset and/or actions you will take to get back on track.

What obstacles might knock you down?	What will you do to get back on the Success Curve?

Don't quit.

Acknowledge the setback and **keep moving forward**.

You've got the time, and the time is NOW.

Earlier, I promised you that if you took the Great Life NOW journey with me, you'd create a Game Plan with prioritized goals and activities that would help you decrease stress, live on purpose, achieve greater optimism and happiness, and be more successful in virtually all areas of your life. You've positioned yourself to own my promise and make it truly your own.

I also mentioned that even though implementing your Game Plan requires a time investment, in the end, you'll potentially save a lot of time.

Think about all the time spent dealing with issues you face in your life today—problems that make moving your mountains feel impossible: career hurdles, relationship issues, poor health and wellness, financial stress, and other struggles that drain productivity and happiness. You've positioned yourself to improve in each of these areas in ways that alleviate stress and SAVE YOU TIME.

As promised, I'm asking again: Will you invest about 3% of your day to ensure the other 97% is truly Great?

> **Champions keep playing until they get it right.**
>
> -Billie Jean King

A quick refresher on the math. You have 1,440 minutes each day. The same as everyone else. Assuming you sleep eight hours a day, that leaves 16 hours (960 minutes) of awake time for living your Great Life NOW.

Remember, we calculate that, on average, you have 960 minutes each day. 3% of that is approximately 30 minutes. That's it!

16 hours awake
x 60 minutes per hour
960 minutes each day

3% of 960 minutes is about 30 minutes. These 30 minutes are a gift for you to provide yourself each and every day. It's a small amount of time to get you started. You can do it, right? Of course you can. If you couldn't invest a mere 30 minutes each and every day, you would never have made it this far in your Great Life NOW journey.

3% of your time is all you need to invest to be successful implementing your Great Life NOW Game Plan... about 30 minutes a day.

Some of you are thinking, that's it, only 30 minutes? Maybe you could do 45 minutes or an hour or more each day. My recommendation is to begin with 30 minutes. That is where I started and where my clients find the most success. You can always increase it after a few weeks. I increased mine to an hour after the first six months. Recently, I've increased my investment to 90 minutes on most days. I simply get up an hour earlier and leverage the beginning of my day in even more powerful ways, which often includes a morning walk where I can consume content that helps my mind flourish. Please understand, I wasn't a "morning person" before committing to a Great Life NOW.

In fact, like most, I used to love to sleep in and found my buzzing alarm clock beyond annoying. It was downright painful on most days as I dragged my ass out of bed and started my day with a mindset of uneasiness, stress, and worry.

Years ago, I forced myself to become a morning person out of necessity. Why? Because there never seemed to be enough time in the day. So, I began getting up earlier, often by 5 a.m., to get a jump on my to-do list. What I found was that I was simply working more hours, adding to my stress and my physical and mental exhaustion without necessarily getting more work done and certainly without being more productive. I was busier than ever.

I learned that I was making the same mistake many people make in thinking they are being productive because they are busy and working a lot of hours. I was confusing being busy with being productive. I glorified being busy and felt as if downtime was wasted time. Boy, was I wrong.

I soon realized being productive and being busy and working a lot are not necessarily correlated.

Being busy doing things doesn't create success, doing the right things does.

Working hard doesn't create as much success as working smarter. And if you're doing the wrong things, doing more of them won't increase your odds of success. In fact, in some cases, they just help you to fail faster. While I was not feeling as if I was failing, I knew for certain that I wasn't really focused on working smarter, not harder.

Deploying your ½ Hour of Power with two Universal Habits.

INVEST IN A ½ HOUR OF POWER!

You are ready to activate your Game Plan. There are no excuses. The time is NOW and you have all the ingredients for success. You have your Superpowers. You defined The Brand Called YOU, determined your Empowering Beliefs, analyzed and prioritized your focus areas to move your Mountains for Growth, and created goals and habits that will catapult you up the Success Curve.

Your last step on this journey is to commit to your ½ Hour of Power with two additional habits that will complement your work thus far:

1. **Determine Your Daily Top Five.**
2. **Meditate to Reflect, Refocus, and Reenergize**.

I call them Universal Habits because they work for EVERYONE to create motivation, instill confidence, and help them get their day off to a great start. It doesn't matter what your focus areas or goals are… these two habits will help you create the positive energy and momentum needed to achieve them. And, best of all, they only take up some of your ½ Hour of Power.

Determine **Your Daily Top Five.**

You have a lot of stuff to get done. You have your goals and newly minted habits in place, and it may feel like you've added even more to your already busy day. And you may not yet realize exactly what you'll be taking off your plate in the future. (You may not have come to the realization that making progress on your habits and getting closer to your goals will actually save you time. Wait for it, it's coming.)

Now, it's time to put your Game Plan into action with the Daily Top Five approach to managing your to-do list.

I was inspired to create and master this Universal Habit after reading a quote from Norman Vincent Peale, the American minister and author best known for popularizing the concept of positive thinking.[12] In fact, in 1952, Peale wrote the bestseller *The Power of Positive Thinking*, which sold more than five million copies.

So, here's the quote:

"Plan your work for today and every day; THEN work your plan."

Simple, right? To demonstrate this habit, all you need is a small piece of paper to write down your top five things to accomplish each day. I use a 3 x 5 index card. You may prefer to make a list on your smartphone. The way you do it doesn't matter; what's important is jotting down your priorities and crossing them off as you do them.

Here are the steps to the Daily Top Five Universal Habit.

Before you begin, name it. Sometimes I write, "Get IT Done," and other days I write something more motivational, such as "Crush-It List."

Step 1: Think about your top priorities for the week and list the most important actions to accomplish for that day. Don't worry about the order; that will come in a moment. Simply write down the most important tasks or the strategic project you are working on that you want to make progress on. Include as much detail as you are comfortable with regarding what progress will look like.

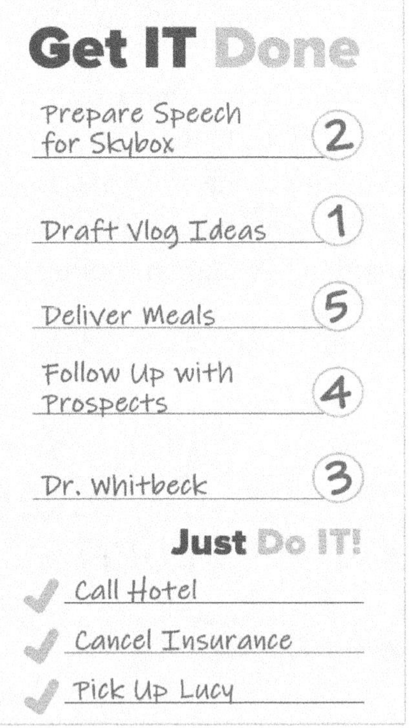

Step 2: At the bottom, jot down your Just Do It items. These are the quick calls or emails that you need to get to at some point. You know, the tasks that weigh you down because you know you need to "just do" them. They are easy to do, but also easy to put off.

By getting these items out of your head, they become less of a distraction during the day. You don't need the extra distraction keeping you from your most important tasks. So, put these tasks in the bottom corner where they will wait to get crossed off. In some cases, you may want to schedule 30 minutes into your day (Time Block) to tackle your Just Do It action items.

Step 3: Prioritize your action items by writing a 1 next to the most important task to begin with. Then identify number 2 and so on. I'll do this for up to five action items each day.

Step 4: Make sure you've time blocked appropriately to get stuff done. If you look at your calendar and see that you don't have the time available, then you'll either need to reschedule something or block the time for a future date. Don't allow important tasks on your list without also having the time to do them. Doing so only leads to more stress and feelings of failure—not what you are going for. You want to focus, finish, and appreciate your success and progress toward your goals.

There is one final step… but before I share it, here's an even more important piece of advice: Don't start Action Item 2 until Action Item 1 is complete. That's right... tackle each action item in order and avoid multitasking. If you've time blocked appropriately, you shouldn't run into this challenge. Simply stick to your schedule.

I am not saying this is going to be easy, but you can do it. Consider turning off notifications, shutting down email, and maybe even silencing your phone for a while during some of the highest-priority tasks. If you're not willing to do this for an action on your list, well, maybe that activity isn't really all that important.

Okay, here is the fifth and final step.

Step 5: Review and cross off the action items you finish. Actually draw a line through them and take a moment to appreciate your progress. Doing so is going to feel good! Take pride in what you've accomplished. If you are using a smartphone, use whatever is available to cross things off in your app.

Of course, there will be times you simply can't get everything crossed off your list. This is not a problem. Highlight those items, make sure to time block them into your calendar, and they will be waiting for you the next day or sometime in the near future.

By following the Daily Top Five method, you will train your brain to focus your attention and time on your highest priority stuff, and guess what? After investing a few weeks doing this, you will be pleasantly surprised by how easy it becomes to plan your day and work your plan.

Meditation to survive.

I am a recovering anti-meditator. Okay, I've said it. I just needed to confess and get it out in the open. For years, I was that guy who was reluctant to try meditation because not only was I "too busy," I also didn't want to be one of those "meditation types." You know, those free-spirited people who tend to go against the norms (at least what I perceived as the norms) of daily life.

However, my stress level continued to rise, and my health was deteriorating with episodes of kidney stones, anxiety, and lightheadedness. So, I began poking around to learn more about what meditation is and whether it was something I should try. During that process, I learned more about who else had a daily meditation practice. Jerry Seinfeld... Ellen DeGeneres... Wait... those are two of my favorite TV personalities! Lebron James... Michael Jordan... What!?! Now I was curious. What I very quickly realized was that these über-successful people were meditating not just for the immediate, stress-reducing, happiness-generating benefits, but for the future life-altering results they experienced.

I gave it a try yet was stuck on the Failure Curve for many years. I couldn't seem to get myself to meditate consistently, and I kept telling myself the same old lie: I am too busy. Even though I was aware of some of the benefits and could cite many successful people in my network (as well as the famously successful people) who made time to meditate, I still told myself the lie. Have you told yourself this lie?

When the pain of my busyness alongside the incredibly high level of self-induced stress became nearly unbearable, I finally got serious about taking time to calm my mind. But even then, I had not evolved to where I would truly make meditation a habit that would positively change my life.

I'd like to save you the years of inconsistent success marked by periods of failure and help you master this habit of meditation so you can apply it to your Great Life NOW journey.

After years of failing, something happened. My journey from a wannabe to a daily practitioner began with meditation as a technique for survival. At the time, my company, Brand Integrity, had grown significantly. Instead of having a few employees and two or three client engagements going on, we had dozens of consultants and software engineers and 50 or more client engagements going on at any one time. My speaking business was also flourishing, putting me on the road weekly with multi-city engagements to present to large audiences of business leaders. I felt pressure to bring my "A-game" every single time. And while I loved the speaking business, especially the preparation work and being in front of the audience, I quickly tired of the travel and didn't like being away from my family. After several years of this fast-paced, hectic life—running in what I called "fifth gear," doing upward of 80 speeches in a year—I found myself at a point of total burnout and exhaustion.

Meditation became my technique to survive. It became a need-based strategy for me so I could mentally get through the day. Let me be clear, I was not using meditation to thrive, I was just trying to survive.

I began with a morning ritual to meditate between 10 and 20 minutes. I soon realized how much easier this became, and I was actually enjoying it, so I added a second session on some afternoons. Here I was, still running in fifth gear each day, but I'd successfully put a band-aid on my mental well-being and was able to increase my focus and productivity with a few sessions of mind-calming daily meditations.

Then something else happened. I achieved a major milestone in my life when I sold Brand Integrity and its employee engagement software program.

Immediately, my stress level dissipated, and I soon found that my entire life shifted from fifth gear to third gear. And let me tell you, it is amazing how clearly you can see when you are in third gear.

It's amazing how clearly you can see when you are in third gear.

I had more clarity regarding my priorities than ever before. For the first time in my career, I was able to focus my time and energy on the few parts of my work that I loved most: coaching, speaking, and consulting. I now had more time to myself and more time than ever with my family. I was on cloud nine, truly enjoying life. But that didn't last long. One other thing changed. I stopped consistently meditating. I went from daily meditation to once a week or less. Why? Because I no longer felt the stress that led me to meditate to survive. I told myself: I am in third gear now, and I have such clarity on where I want to focus.

However, while I was no longer suffering from the pressure and stress of running Brand Integrity, supporting dozens of families and hundreds of clients in any given year, I still did not feel like I was thriving. Even though I had mastered the Universal Habit of my Daily Top Five, something was missing.

My morning ½ Hour of Power routine was quick and got me off to a good start. But I knew I could do better. I was working my Great Life NOW Game Plan, and good was not going to cut it. I needed to be great. And to make my mornings great, I needed to find a way to make meditation truly habitual.

Meditation to thrive.

Being curious about why I'd fallen off the meditation wagon and knowing I needed to strengthen my WHY for the habit of meditation, I began to research the benefits. I discovered two biological facts that convinced me (and now hopefully you) to take decisive action to commit to the Universal Habit of meditation, not as a survival technique but to help me thrive.

Two biological facts about meditation.

FACT #1: Meditation makes your brain more efficient (and maybe smarter).

Scientists have proven that meditation has a significant effect on your work and personal performance.[13] Why? Because it rewires your brain to be more efficient. The medical term is neuroplasticity, which is a fancy word for the brain's ability to change itself. The brain can become more effective, in turn allowing you to be more innovative, creative, and a better problem solver.

Let's get even more specific. Meditation increases the gray and white matter in your brain as it enlarges the structure that connects the right and left hemispheres. If you look at the human brain, you'll see that the size and shape of the right and left hemispheres are perfectly balanced. And the white matter between them is a C-shaped structure called the corpus callosum. The corpus callosum enables communication and interaction between the two sides.

Scientists have determined that when we meditate, we are providing the corpus callosum a workout, enabling it to strengthen. The longer you have a meditation practice, the thicker the corpus callosum becomes, just like any other muscle you put through a workout. Researchers have uncovered that meditation can change the brain enough to be visibly detectable by an MRI in only two months!

This stronger connection between the analytical and intuitive hemispheres (your critical mind and your creative mind) helps your brain work in true harmony, communicating more effectively and, in the words of some scientists, "making you smarter." That's right, there is a significant body of research saying that when you strengthen the corpus callosum through meditation, you actually become smarter. I figure if I can invest a short amount of time (10 to 20 minutes) a day, and it will make me smarter, then I'd be crazy not to.

As if you needed any more incentive than having a more efficient brain and becoming smarter, scientists have also concluded that a regular practice of meditation makes you younger (or at least makes your brain appear younger). Evidence shows that regular meditation keeps the brain up to 20 years younger than the brains of those who do not regularly practice meditation. Smarter and younger... let's do this!

FACT #2: Meditation can rescue you from the bully of stress.

Let's face it, stress is a bully that keeps your mind trapped in a constant state of unrest, worry, and discontent. Like a playground bully, stress keeps you looking over your shoulder and feeling on edge... and it deteriorates your focus and productivity.

It's not bad to get stressed, but it is bad to stay stressed. This is where meditation comes to the rescue.

Meditation affects the body in exactly the opposite ways that stress does by triggering the body's relaxation response. It restores the body to a calm state, helping the body repair itself while preventing new damage from the physical effects of stress. Not sure what I mean by damage? Take a look at the before and after pictures of any president from inauguration day to the day they left office. After four (or eight) years of carrying the weight of the world on their shoulders, they invariably look older, grayer, and more tired. The constant demands, sleepless nights, and unending responsibilities all add up to a perfect storm of rapidly accumulating stress and a rapidly aging body.

You may not have the stress of the president, but do you have high demands, a few restless nights of sleep each week, and a Raging River of Responsibilities? Then you have a bully to confront—and meditation can help.

When you meditate, you "de-excite" your nervous system, which decreases your metabolic rate, helping you get rid of stress from your past. When you "de-excite" your nervous system, you enable it to purge old stress from the body in a far more efficient manner, paving the way for better performance and mental clarity. It's that simple. You slow down, become calmer, and open yourself up to greater clarity. This calmness and mental clarity have also been shown to improve the immune system. As if combating the stress bully wasn't enough of a benefit, you can also calm your nervous system and reinvigorate your immune system so it will be ready to act when you need it.

You can't eliminate stress from your life, but you can take steps to train your mind to better adapt to whatever comes your way. When you do this, you will be managing stress instead of letting stress manage you, and your brain and body will recapture the energy that was being absorbed by fear-based thinking.

You can seize the energy you are wasting on being fearful and repurpose it into more positive thinking and actions that help you live a Great Life NOW.

I've now made the habit of meditation a regular practice. I don't claim to be an expert or even all that good at it. And every now and then I land on the Failure Curve, struggling to be as consistent as I'd like to be. However, for the most part, I've been quite disciplined in making it a part of my routine and am reaping the rewards.

I often enjoy guided meditations, using some of my favorite apps such as Calm, Insight Timer, Brain.fm, or Headspace. Other times, I will sit and breathe, thinking of absolutely nothing other than a mantra that is meaningful to me. I've found with meditation that variety really is the spice of life, and many people get bored with the same approach over and over. So, if you're having trouble making meditation a habit, my advice to you is to mix it up and try different ways to engage your heart and mind, and over time you will determine what works best.

The End Is Just the Beginning.

We began this journey together with me guaranteeing you'd learn the recipe for a Great Life. I said, "All you've got to do is bring the motivation."

You've learned the recipe. You've created the Great Life NOW Game Plan.

You've examined what makes you happy and what fears get in the way of helping you achieve what you want most in life. You've determined your Purpose, uncovered your Strengths, and taken a deep dive into the Brand Called YOU. You've made your core values "visible" by defining the behaviors required to live them, every day! You've explored the Mountains for Growth and figured out which ones are most important to you right NOW. Lastly, you've outlined your highest priority goals and the mission-critical THINKING and DOING habits you will make progress on in the days, weeks, months, and years ahead.

NOW is the time to harness your motivation and activate your game plan.

Remember when I shared with you the story about my mom and the letter she left me. Recall that I made a promise to you. I said, "I didn't know at the time that her words would have such a significant impact on my life and subsequently, on the lives of many others. And soon, they will have an impact on you too."

My mom said, "Once you have self-worth, you can move mountains." At 12 years old, this grabbed my attention and became a guiding principle for how to live my life.

However, I've gleaned more insights that I've used to harness my energy and create the necessary focus to execute my game plan. I've organized the insights into Four Truths that will do the same for you.

If you embrace and implement these Four Truths, there will be no stopping you. You will hit the ground running with the implementation of your Great Life NOW Game Plan.

The Four Truths to Implementing Your Great Life NOW Game Plan.

The First Truth: You Make the Rules.

Remember, life is a game we are all playing and to play the game successfully, you must know your rules. You make the rules by defining WHO you are and HOW you want to live it. Moving forward, how you think about these rules, how often you think about them, and how you act them out represents you "following your rules."

In her letter to me and my brother, my mom said, "Once you have self-worth, you can move mountains." However, the very next sentence provided even more direction. "Whatever price you have to pay, pay it!!" She used two exclamation points to emphasize how important this message was. I took notice. She indicated that self-worth was a feeling of being self-assured, of knowing WHO you are and being happy with WHO you are. You've figured this out for yourself. You've completed the upfront work, you've become more self-assured and determined how you need to think and act to win in this game of life; therefore, you can't lose, as long as you know your rules, believe in your rules, and, most importantly, play by your rules.

Whatever price you have to pay,
pay it!!

Where else in life do you get to make up the rules? Nowhere. But you do in this game called "life." Imagine if you got to make the rules in other games. In a track meet, what if you got to start five seconds before the other runners? How about if in the game of Monopoly, you got two pieces of real estate every time your opponents earned one? You'd win every time, wouldn't you? Of course you would. Nowhere else in your day-to-day existence do you get to make up the rules to influence your success. This means you can't lose if you believe in the Brand Called YOU and follow the rules you've outlined for how to think, speak, and act.

Recall the insight about the power of your mindset and beliefs: The one thing you have complete control over in your life is what you think about.

You've documented your core values to guide what you are going to think about and how you are going to act in the future. You've determined the goals you want to achieve to move your mountains forward. NOW, all you must do is "mind your thoughts" each and every day.

How are you going to do this? The answer lies in the next three truths.

The Second Truth: You've Got Lots of Time.

When you began this journey, you determined how many days you've lived and how many you believe you have left. Think back to how many days you may have left. It's a lot, isn't it?

My mom only got 11,957 days. Some of you have more time left than she had in her lifetime. She was not bitter about this. In fact, she said, "I hold no resentment for what life has dealt me—I fully understand because I have grown. So many people stop growing so young—it's a bore and a waste. But if you get the most out of everything you see, do, and experience, it's all worthwhile."

She also said, "Life is not easy; so much has to do with your attitudes and actions and what you do with the hours, days, and years. They all equal LIFE!"

Her message was clear. Time is one of your most precious resources. It's finite. Use it wisely.

When I say you've got lots of time, how does that make you feel? When I share this Second Truth from the stage, my audiences stare at me with a combination of disbelief and doubt. Some look as if they want to call bullshit on me. I'll typically wait a few seconds to allow the truth to sink in.

Then I prove it to them, just as I will for you.

The reality is, our lives are quite simple. Your life is quite simple. You've got three buckets of time: Sleep, Work, and Everything Else.

For illustration purposes, I'll make assumptions in the following examples.

Sleep Bucket: A healthy individual will sleep between six to eight hours per day. Let's assume you average eight hours a night. That would be quite healthy, wouldn't it? For this exercise, go ahead and grant yourself the maximum sleep of eight hours.

Work Bucket: Let's assume you are working 50 hours each week. Most of us don't, even though some say they do. However, let's be assumptive here and make sure you don't understate your work hours. By the way, your work doesn't have to be a paid job. Maybe you volunteer or care for a family member, or have an important hobby. Put this allocation of time into your "work" bucket.

So, now you've used up 106 hours of the week. That leaves an additional 62 hours that will go into your third bucket: the Everything Else Bucket.

Everything Else Bucket: This bucket of 62 hours each week can hold everything else you want to get done while you are awake and not working. This is a lot of time each week. You've got your go-to activities, such as: watch TV, shop, cook, eat, exercise, read, and a host of other social and community related stuff. However, let's be honest: In any given week, there is plenty of time for you to invest in your Great Life NOW Game Plan. You need to allocate this time just like any other precious resource.

Too often, well intentioned people witness constant imbalances, often feeling as if they are not getting enough done. They end the day exhausted and feeling as if they didn't have enough time.

From my experience, those sliding down the Failure Curve become extremely busy with being productive. These people glorify their busyness and falsely believe they have a time problem. They believe the Raging River of Responsibility is prohibiting them from making the progress they desire. The reality is, they don't have a time problem. They have a motivation and priority challenge.

Here is what I've learned about those who live a great life and those who don't: One of the main differences is how people invest their time.

Regardless of how much money you have, where you live, and what you do for a living, you only get 168 hours each week. That's it. You can't buy, beg for, or bribe for extra time.

Therefore, how you use your 168 hours makes all the difference in the world between struggling on the Failure Curve versus a gradual climb up the Success Curve.

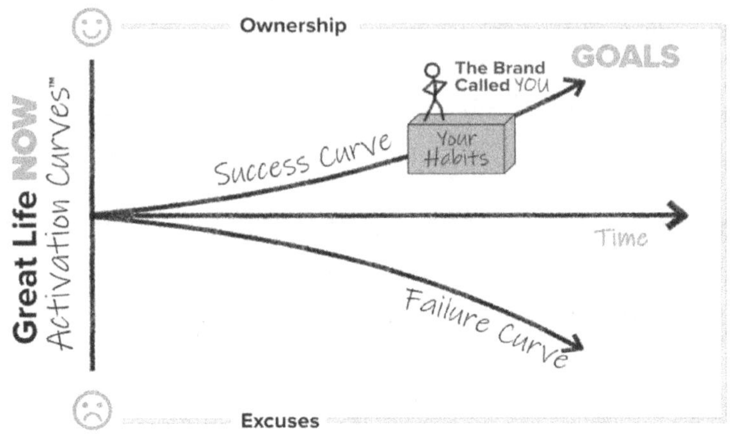

Remember, you've got the time. As you will see in this next exercise, you have lots of time.

You don't have a time problem; you have a motivation and priority challenge.

When facilitating this exercise, I typically witness two responses. For some, the concept immediately resonates because they know they suffer from a "priority challenge," yet have disguised it as a time problem. Their experience is a lack of balance, which impacts their energy and focus.

For others, they are surprised and a bit more curious—as if they've never really thought about this before. For me, it has been natural, as I've obsessed over time management my entire adult life. In my early twenties, I posted a sign on my bathroom mirror that read, "You've got 1440 minutes today. Use them wisely." So of course, the idea of breaking the week into hours and determining how to deploy them came naturally. But I realize this is a new concept for some. The concept is easy. 24 hours a day multiplied by seven days in a week equals 168 hours. That's all I get. That's all you get.

The difficult part is admitting we have the time to do what is most important to us. Admitting we do have the time to move those mountains.

As you will see, you've got lots of time!

You just have to do some research to figure out where it is hiding.

This next exercise will help you find it.

In your workbook . . .

Investigate for Hidden Time.

Step 1: Find the hidden time.

- For an entire week, every 30 – 60 minutes, jot down how you spend your time. List specific activities. If after one week you've not found a great deal of hidden time, do it a second week.

Step 2: Time Block your priorities.

- At the beginning of each week (or at the end of each week) make a list of your top priorities. Consider your Mountains for Growth when making your priorities.
- Review your calendar and Time Block those highest priorities. If you are most productive in the morning, be sure to block accordingly.
- If you must encroach on a blocked time, then reschedule it immediately. Do not cancel on your high priorities.

Not every week will be on target. Your goal is to balance the 168 hours by keeping track of how you are spending your time and to hold yourself accountable to living your brand and doing the habits to move your mountains.

The Third Truth: Your Habits Cause Your Happiness.

My mom said, "Life is not easy. So much has to do with your attitudes and actions." This brings us to the Third Truth: Your Habits Cause Your Happiness and Success.

Once again, habits are nothing more than thoughts and actions repeated over and over until they become second nature. Your life consists of two types of habits: thinking and doing.

Earlier you learned the five-step process for activating any goal and habit in your life. Here is a short summary:

Step 1: Describe what you want. In this step, document the actions and results you want to see happen. Write down the goals you are trying to achieve.

Step 2: Know your WHY. If you want to make progress moving your mountains and achieving your goals, you'll want to know doing so will make a positive difference in your life and/or the lives of others.

Step 3: Design the habits. Remember, a Great Life NOW doesn't happen by chance, it happens by design. Write out the thoughts and actions required to do your desired habits.

Step 4: Demonstrate staying power. Predict where and when you might run out of willpower and document the thoughts and actions that will keep you on track.

Step 5: Ask every day, "Did I try?" Each day, invest a few seconds to ask yourself whether you tried to do the habits you've committed to. Don't ask whether you did it. Just ask whether you tried. If the habit is important to you, you won't keep lying to yourself, and the pressure of having to answer to yourself will help push you down the pathway of progress. I recommend downloading a habit tracking app on your phone and setting an alarm each day to remind you to ask yourself if you tried.

Once you commit to the Habit Activation Process and work through it a few times, it too will become habitual, making it easier and easier to set, track, and successfully implement habits. You should begin with one or two habits and then work your way up to several at a time. As I think back to when I began using the Habit Activation Process, I started with one habit, then took on another, then two more, and before I knew it, I was working through a dozen different habits in any given year, turning most of them into second nature ways of thinking and doing.

That's the kind of progress you will make when you commit to living by the Third Truth: Your Habits Cause Your Happiness and Success.

In the last section, you embraced two Universal Habits.

1. **Determine Your Daily Top Five**

2. **Meditate to Reflect, Refocus, and Reenergize**

In addition, you've outlined a number of habits that will bring the Brand Called YOU to life, while helping you to move your mountains forward, achieving your stated goals.

What you are about to learn and put into practice is one more habit that will power all others.

Speak My Daily Commitments.

The Speak My Daily Commitment habit will put you on the Success Curve by igniting the "thinking system" that drives your mindset and attitude. This habit is simple to do. Just speak your commitment each day. You will quickly see that your voice has tremendous influence over your attitude and actions.

In this final exercise, you will use your voice to speak your intentions, reminding you of who you are and how you live it. You will see that verbalizing what is important to you is considerably more powerful than typing or writing. You'll notice your voice infuses deeper meaning and commitment to the Brand Called You: the mountains you want to move, what you are grateful for, and the goals you want to make progress toward achieving.

Warning: Do not even think of skipping the Speak My Daily Commitment. Doing so will have predictable consequences. If you try to activate your Game Plan without this daily commitment to your intentions, you'll risk sliding down the Failure Curve. To help you, make sure you use the Habit Activation Process above.

I realize that many people will think this effort is hokey and maybe even a little uncomfortable. If this is you, then you'll need to get comfortable with being a little uncomfortable. I promise you, it won't last. It will become natural for you once you make it a habit.

The Universe does reward attitude and action. However, that action must be intentional, and intentionality comes from a "trained mindset" that you have complete control over. It's your job to train it. That training starts NOW by speaking to yourself your Daily Commitment.

In your workbook . . .

Speak My Daily Commitments.

Complete each section of the Daily Commitment and then at least once per day, speak it out loud or quietly in your mind. Out loud will have more impact. Doing this once a day is good. Twice a day is better. And make sure to track your progress on your phone with your chosen habit tracking app.

Here are a few tips to get you started:

- **Complete each section of the Daily Commitments.** Choose your words carefully. Bring as much emotion and conviction into the words as you can.

- **Speak with confidence and conviction.** Something magical happens when you ignite this daily conversation and do so out loud. I promise you, after you do it a few times, it won't feel as weird as it sounds.

- **Find a space that is comfortable for you.** Any space where you can focus and be comfortable.

• **Do it daily** (twice daily for maximum benefit). When you wake, speak your Daily Commitments. Before you go to bed, do it again. And if you get the chance in between, do it then too. Make speaking your commitments a “doing” habit that will bring your values to life and help you move your mountains.

• **Let the Universe handle the outcomes.** If you believe that the Universe rewards attitude and action, then let that powerful voice of yours be the guide, and don't stress out about the future outcome. You've declared your intentions and commitments. It has been said. Let it be done.

As you can imagine, there are many inspiring thoughts and intentions that can go into your Daily Commitments. Begin with the basics from your Great Life NOW Game Plan. Start with the Brand Called Me, and based on the core values you’ve created, write out an “I am” statement. Feel free to include additional detail that inspires you.

Next, if you’ve found your Purpose statement to be meaningful, then consider including it as well.

Review your Mountains for Growth and include a bullet point for each of your high-priority intentions.

Lastly, include what you are most grateful for. Consider those ideas that tend to come up regularly—family, health, friends, career, etc.

When you first build out your Daily Commitments, you may only have a few ideas in each category, and it may only take you about 20 seconds to read each day. As you continue to grow as a human and make progress living your Great Life NOW Game Plan, you may decide to add a few more ideas. My Daily Commitment has been modified dozens of times as I continuously look to keep it fresh and enhance its meaning. What doesn’t tend to change very often are the core values that make up the Brand Called Me. However, every now and then, what I am most grateful for and my intentions for moving my mountains are modified.

Do what makes the most sense to you. You are the one who must adopt it, think it, speak it, and live it every day!

In your workbook . . .

The Recommended Framework for the Daily Commitments

My Commitments and Declarations

I am (YOUR NAME)

I am The Brand Called ME:

-
-
-
-

My Purpose is to:

-

My intentions to move my Mountains for Growth:

-
-

I am grateful for:

-
-

The Fourth Truth: NOW!

Once again, life is happening right NOW!

My mom made the investment to write that letter to me and Andy. She could have put it off. But she didn't. If she had, she most likely would have been too weak to share the incredible insights the way she did.

All of us have important things to do that will improve our lives. There is a starting point for everything. And the time for you is NOW!

Recall from the beginning of our time together, I shared my observation that about 1 in 20 people (5%) are living a Great Life NOW—meaning they are truly living with healthy (and manageable) amounts of stress, an abundance of happiness, and a day-to-day feeling of being successful. Not just success as measured in wealth or status, but the kind of success that comes from a life filled with healthy relationships, where they enjoy their work, love their family, and like and respect themselves. The kind of life where people have the right mindset and take the right actions that fuel their self-worth and guide them to make progress on achieving their goals.

When you first read this, you may have wondered how my observation could be so low. Well, first off, most people have never gone on a journey like the Great Life NOW. And many of those that do, don't implement The Fourth Truth. And without it, nothing else matters.

For decades, I've focused in on what makes the difference between those who are living a great life and those who are not. Why do some continue to struggle to get fit, strengthen relationships, manage their mindsets, and take their careers and finances to higher grounds?

Action makes the difference.

People need a simple system with easy strategies to focus on the actions that drive results. Make no mistake, there will not be consistent results without consistent action.

To live a Great Life, you have to take action every day. You have to do what people living great lives do. You've outlined it beautifully. You've just got to do it. Remember, successful people do what unsuccessful people are not willing to do.

You no longer have time as an excuse. The Truth is... your time is NOW.

Go move your mountains.

ABOUT THE AUTHOR

Gregg Lederman is a New York Times, USA Today, and Wall Street Journal bestselling author of three award-winning books that leaders of values-driven organizations have used to create incredibly high employee engagement.

As an entrepreneur, Gregg has built and sold several companies while also serving for two decades as an adjunct professor at the University of Rochester Simon School of Business where he has guided executive MBAs on the journey to living a **Great Life NOW**.

As a coach, speaker, and consultant, Gregg has worked with thousands of organizations and their leaders to create happier, more motivated, and productive workforces.

Gregg lives in Rochester, New York, with his wife, Karyn, three daughters, and dogs, Milo and Rocky. If you'd like more information on Gregg, his books, or his coaching and speaking events, visit **gregglederman.com.**

NOTES

WELCOME

1. Sifferlin, A. (2017, July 26). Here's How Happy Americans Are Right Now: Harris Poll. Retrieved March 14, 2021, from https://time.com/4871720/how-happy-are-americans/
2. Chokshi, N. (2019, April 25). Americans Are Among the Most Stressed People in the World, Poll Finds. Retrieved March 14, 2021, from https://www.nytimes.com/2019/04/25/us/americans-stressful.html
3. Wanderlust Worker. (2020, June 18). The Harvard MBA Business School Study on Goal Setting. Retrieved March 14, 2021, from https://www.wanderlustworker.com/the-harvard-mba-business-school-study-on-goal-setting/
4. Faith Hope & Psychology. (2012, April 30). 80% of Thoughts Are Negative... 95% Are Repetitive. Retrieved March 14, 2021, from https://faithhopeandpsychology.wordpress.com/2012/03/02/80-of-thoughts-are-negative-95-are-repetitive/

PART 1: PREGAME

1. Helliwell, J., Layard, R., & Sachs, J., et. al. (2022). World Happiness Report 2022. Retrieved May 9, 2022, from https://worldhappiness.report/ed/2022/
2. Pursuit of Happiness. (2021). Aristotle and His Definition of Happiness. Retrieved March 19, 2021, from https://www.pursuit-of-happiness.org/history-of-happiness/aristotle/
3. Lyubomirsky, S. (2008). *The How of Happiness: A Scientific Approach to Getting the Life You Want.* New York, NY: Penguin Press.
4. Carnegie, D. (1984). *How to Stop Worrying and Start Living.* New York, NY: Simon &; Schuster.
5. Roach, A. R., Salt, C. E., & Segerstrom, S. C. (2009). Generalizability of Repetitive Thought: Examining Stability in Thought Content and Process. *Cognitive Therapy and Research*, 34(2), 144-158. doi:10.1007/s10608-009-9232-3

6. Singh, O. (2020, May 26). Chris Evans Says His Anxiety and Panic Attacks Led Him to Turn Down His Role as Captain America Before Eventually Accepting. Retrieved March 14, 2021, from https://www.insider.com/chris-evans-captain-america-turned-down-marvel-anxiety-panic-attacks-2020-5

PART 2: THE GAME PLAN

1. Houle, B. (2020, July 20). An Effective Strengths Program: Cardinal Health Case Study. Retrieved March 14, 2021, from https://www.gallup.com/workplace/236588/effective-strengths-program-cardinal-health-case-study.aspx
2. Asplund, J., Elliot, G., & Flade, P. (2020, November 05). Employees Who Use Their Strengths Outperform Those Who Don't. Retrieved March 14, 2021, from https://www.gallup.com/workplace/236561/employees-strengths-outperform-don.aspx
3. *Amazingly Simple Theory for a Happy Life* [Video file]. (2017, February 22). Retrieved March 14, 2021, from https://www.youtube.com/watch?v=uTkvEUwYfpY

PART 3: ACTIVATING THE GAME PLAN

1. Antanaityte, N. (n.d.). Mind Matters: How to Effortlessly Have More Positive Thoughts. Retrieved March 14, 2021, from https://tlexinstitute.com/how-to-effortlessly-have-more-positive-thoughts/
2. Singer, M. A. (2013). *The Untethered Soul: The Journey Beyond Yourself.* Oakland, CA: New Harbinger Publications.
3. Thorp, C. (2021, March 11). Four Noble Truths. Retrieved March 14, 2021, from https://www.ancient.eu/Four_Noble_Truths/
4. Locke, E. A. (2005). Setting Goals for Life and Happiness. In *Oxford Handbook of Positive Psychology* (pp. 299-312). Oxford, UK: Oxford University Press.
5. Wood, W., & Neal, D. T. (2009, October 2). The Habitual Consumer. Retrieved March 14, 2021, from https://dornsife.usc.edu/assets/sites/545/docs/Wendy_Wood_Research_Articles/H abits/wood.neal.2009._the_habitual_consumer.pdf
6. University of North Carolina. (2020, December 14). Changing Habits. Retrieved March 15, 2021, from https://learningcenter.unc.edu/tips-and-tools/changing-habits/

7. Isaacson, W. (2003). *Benjamin Franklin: An American Life*. New York, NY: Thorndike Press.

8. Fretts, B. (2013, December 23). TV Guide Magazine's 60 Best Series of All Time. Retrieved March 15, 2021, from https://www.tvguide.com/news/tv-guide-magazine-60-best-series-1074962/

9. Polivy, J., & Herman, C. P. (1985). Dieting and Binging: A Causal Analysis. *American Psychologist*, 40(2), 193-201. doi:10.1037/0003-066x.40.2.193

10. McGonigal, K. (2013). *The Willpower Instinct*. New York, NY: Avery.

11. Tracy, B. (2015, May 11). Making Course Corrections. Retrieved March 15, 2021, from https://www.briantracy.com/blog/brians-words-of-wisdom/making-course-corrections/

12. Peale, N. V. (2005). *The Power of Positive Thinking: The Amazing Results of Positive Thinking*. New York, NY: Simon & Schuster.

13. Sage, L. (2020, July 31). Council Post: Six Proven Benefits of Meditation in the Workplace. Retrieved March 15, 2021, from https://www.forbes.com/sites/forbesbusinesscouncil/2020/08/03/six-proven-benefits-of-meditation-in-the-workplace/?sh=34606514fa88

www.ingramcontent.com/pod-product-compliance
Lightning Source LLC
LaVergne TN
LVHW010656110826
845149LV00014B/3115

9798998696909